CHESTERTON ON SHAKESPEARE

By the same author
Uniform with this edition

THE SPICE OF LIFE
TREMENDOUS TRIFLES
A MISCELLANY OF MEN
ALL THINGS CONSIDERED

*

Uniform volumes in the
G. K. CHESTERTON REPRINT SERIES

THE CLUB OF QUEER TRADES
THE MAN WHO KNEW TOO MUCH
MANALIVE
FOUR FAULTLESS FELONS
THE POET AND THE LUNATICS
TALES OF THE LONG BOW
THE RETURN OF DON QUIXOTE
THE PARADOXES OF MR. POND
THE BALL AND THE CROSS
THE MAN WHO WAS THURSDAY
THE NAPOLEON OF NOTTING HILL

CHESTERTON ON SHAKESPEARE

G. K. CHESTERTON

Edited by Dorothy Collins
Introduction by John Sullivan

DUFOUR EDITIONS, INC.

First published 1971

Copyright © Dorothy E. Collins

Library of Congress Catalog Card
Number 79-176309

Set in 11 on 12pt Baskerville

PRINTED IN GREAT BRITAIN
FOR DUFOUR EDITIONS, INC.

Contents

Introduction

The title of this book, echoing as it does Sir Walter Raleigh's deservedly popular *Johnson on Shakespeare*, may seem presumptuous. It is certainly true that Johnson devoted more years to the study of Shakespeare than Chesterton devoted days; that Johnson produced his great edition of Shakespeare and Chesterton wrote no single substantial work on Shakespeare. Nevertheless, there are parallels. Raleigh's observation that Johnson's knowledge of English literature cannot compare with the knowledge of Theobald and Malone can be said of Chesterton as well, indeed has *been* said by Chesterton himself. And the further observation that Johnson undertook no special course of study for his writing on Shakespeare is only too true of Chesterton also. Like Johnson, Chesterton was simply a working man of letters who turned the searchlight of his fine mind on the products of our greatest dramatic poet for the delectation of his readers.

It is now some years since William Empson, in his seminal work of literary criticism, *Seven Types of Ambiguity*, made a passing reference to Chesterton on Shakespeare which betrays the ambivalence (or more properly, perhaps, the ambiguity) of the attitude of the professional literary critic towards the literary journalist. Professor Empson, discussing the line in *Henry V, Part I*,

"The singing masons building roofs of gold"

has a footnote:

"G. K. Chesterton has praised this line, *I think in one of his detective stories*. He had great powers as a verbal critic, *shown mainly be incidental remarks*, and I ought to have acknowledged how much I was using them."

7

The passages I have italicized speak for themselves. That Chesterton's criticism, verbal or otherwise, was not confined to odd remarks in unlikely places is recognized to the full by W. H. Auden in *G. K. Chesterton. A selection from his non-fictional prose* (Faber & Faber, 1970). Introducing his selections from fifteen of Chesterton's books, Mr. Auden remarks that Chesterton's literary criticism "abounds in observations which, once they have been made, seem so obviously true that one cannot understand why one had not seen them for oneself. It now seems obvious to us all . . . that the Elizabethan Age, however brilliant, was not 'spacious', but in literature an age of conceits, in politics an age of conspiracies. But Chesterton was the first critic to see these things. As a literary critic, therefore, I rate him very high."

With no pretensions to scholarship, Chesterton produced among masses of other work covering most areas of literature (and including drama) substantial studies of Browning, Dickens, Cobbett, Stevenson and Chaucer; but he wrote no sustained work on Shakespeare. Such a book was planned, one of the many that were promised and came to nothing. However, scattered through his enormous and varied output are numerous references to Shakespeare and, from time to time, some aspect of Shakespeare was the theme for an essay, a review, an introduction to a book. Dorothy Collins has now made a selection of these writings which provides rather more than a suggestion of Chesterton's approach to Shakespeare and of what we might have had if the major work had ever been written. Spanning his writing life from 1907 to 1935, these pieces range over the tragedies and the comedies, the characters and the criticism, the Baconian heresy and the Shavian controversy, the staging of the plays, and kindred topics. Chesterton was no "words-on-the page" man: he was not concerned with how many children had Lady Macbeth. These essays have the Chestertonian characteristic of seeing their subject from an original angle. It is not to be forgotten that Chesterton, though not an

8

academic critic of the drama was, among his many accomplishments, a playwright himself with *Magic* and *The Judgment of Dr. Johnson* to his credit. This first-hand acquaintance with the theatre gave him an advantage which the cloistered literary critic often lacks.

Bernard Shaw recognized this quality in Chesterton and frequently urged him to write more for the theatre. In this connection, it is interesting to read the two Shaw/Shakespeare essays in this volume, separated in time by nearly a quarter of a century. In *The Great Shawkspear Mystery* Chesterton explains that Shaw, far from being too flippant in his "greater than Shakespeare" pose, is really too serious, too austere, too fanatical, fully to enjoy Shakespeare. Moreover, Shaw lacks poetic insight without which he can never properly appreciate Shakespeare. "The aim of good prose words is to mean what they say. The aim of good poetical words is to mean what they do not say. When Shakespeare says . . .

> 'For valour, is not Love a Hercules,
> Still climbing trees in the Hesperides?'

it is difficult or rather impossible to use any other language to express what he conveys." In the later essay, *Shakespeare and Shaw* Chesterton makes the same point in a different way and in the course of his argument places both Shakespeare and Shaw each in his contemporary setting.

Chesterton sees Shakespeare as a man of the theatre, as actor and playwright, as poet, as a writer of thrillers, as a man of the late Renaissance of whom very little is known. He has no time for Bardolatry and dismisses the Baconians with: "The sane man who is sane enough to see that Shakespeare wrote Shakespeare is sane enough not to worry whether he did or not."

It is good to have these delightful pieces brought together in one volume. That the author of *Browning* and *Charles Dickens* did not produce his projected work on Shakespeare is our loss: we may now, however, find some compensation in seeing *The Macbeths* or *A Midsummer Night's Dream* in a new light and at the same time recognize what we might have had in the larger work denied us.

John Sullivan

Strawberry Hill, 1970

Part One: Set in a Silver Sea

English Literature and the Latin Tradition

I fear the title I have chosen is what we should call a priggish title; that is, a pompous and pedantic title. The world has always rightly rebuked even a scholar when he appeared as a pedant; and it may well regard with reasonable derision a pedant who is not even a scholar. As will appear only too clearly as I proceed, I make no remote claim to classical scholarship; and it may well be asked why I should label this essay with the name of classicism.

What I would here advance, very broadly, is this thesis: first, that the English are not barbarians; second, that the division between England and Europe has been enormously exaggerated. I admit it has sometimes been exaggerated by the English. But that is because, quite lately, England was dominated not only by the English who were ignorant of Europe, but rather specially by the English who were ignorant of England. For my main thesis may appear more of a paradox. I want specially to insist that the classical tradition, the Latin and Greek tradition in English history was the popular thing, the common thing; even the vulgar thing. All those three words, "common" and "popular" and "vulgar", are Latin words. I do not know whether the Anglo-Saxons even had a word for vulgar; the real modern Anglo-Saxons are much too refined. A culture must never be judged by its cultured people. The Latin culture lives in Britain in the uncultured people. It is not a question of English scholars who know Latin. Kamchatkan scholars know Latin; and if there are any Esquimaux scholars, of course they know Latin. They know the Latin scientific word for blubber; and possibly write Latin odes to the walrus, addressing him in the vocative as "walre".

The point is not concerned with the learned; they know Latin, and they know they know it. My point is that the populace, the common men know it without knowing it. Even the old yokel who said, "I ain't no scholar", used a term older than the Schoolmen, as old as the Roman schools. It is not a matter of a Roman pinnacle, but of a Roman pavement. Our populace in every way is such a pavement; and not least in being trampled under foot. For, as I shall try to show, it was the popular Roman tradition that was trampled under foot; and if anything was imposed by aristocrats, it was the pretence of being Anglo-Saxon. Matthew Arnold used the term Barbarian almost as a compliment to an English gentleman; and there was a time quite recently when it was very genteel to be a Barbarian. But it was never very popular, even then, and it had never been heard of before. I wish chiefly to suggest here that it will never be heard of again. The old influence of the southern civilization had sunk so deep in Britain from the beginning, that it was really almost as impossible to weed out the Latin culture from England as to weed it out from Italy. Suppose somebody tried to persuade Italians that their heritage came only from German mercenaries or English trippers or American globe-trotters. Some professors might say that; but it would not be necessary to find more sane and patriotic professors to answer. If these were silent, the very stones would cry out. Not merely the ruins, but the common stones; the stones along the Roman road.

Now, in a much less degree, it is true that the very bones of Britain cried out against the myth that she was barbaric. Our country began as a Roman Province. Popular legend connected it with Brutus, proper history connected it with Caesar. It was such a Province in all common talk and tradition. Only when it ceased to be a Province did it become provincial. It is found not in judgments but in jokes; not in odes but in oaths; in common swear words. I will give one case, because it happens to sum up my thesis. I had a debate with a gentleman who denied all this; he said the English were descended only from Vikings; and could therefore despise all others who were only descended from Roman soldiers or Renaissance artists or such riff-raff. He sent me a huge book refusing all Latin friendship in the title. *By Thor, No!* I delicately evaded reading his book, or the whole of his book; but I said I would prove my whole case merely from the title of the book. I said to him, in effect, "I will give a hundred pounds to the Home for Decayed Vikings, if you can name to me any kind of Englishman, at any period since there have been any kinds of Englishman, who ever in his life said, or even thought of saying, 'By Thor'. But I, on the other hand, will show you thousands and millions of Englishmen, men in clubs, men in pubs, men in trams and trains, ordinary business men grumbling at City dinners, old colonels cursing and swearing on racecourses, all sorts of perfectly ordinary Englishmen, who have habitually said, and do still sometimes say, 'By Jove'." That is the real story of English literature and life; since Caesar, before or after his British adventure, must have gone up to the throne of the Thunderer upon the Rock of the Capitol. *De Jova Principium*; the song began from Jove.

Let me give some examples. The point is that the classic may be found even in the comic; in comic songs and in those patriotic songs that are unfortunately sometimes rather like comic songs. Here is a rude rhyme about St. George and the Dragon, meant to be sung as a drinking-song in the seventeenth century, with a shout for a chorus. Note that it is full of that vagueness about a very remote past, which is the mark of hero-worship by hearsay; the ballad-monger mentions such names as he happens to have heard, heaven knows where.

> Of the deeds done by old kings
>   Is more than I can tell,
> And chiefly of the Romans
>   Who greatly did excel,

> Hannibal and Scipio
> Had many a bloody fight,
> And Orlando Furioso
> Was a very gallant knight.

That is not exactly of marble, in the manner of Racine or Alfieri; but it is classical. It comes out of a people living directly or indirectly on the classics. A rowdy and absurd patriotic song was devoted to the British Grenadiers; but in order to praise those island warriors, it began; "Some talk of Alexander and some of Hercules." In the loneliest inland hamlets, or the dreariest slums of the modern towns, English children can still be found playing a singing-game, with the chorus; "For we are the Romans". Thus, the great legend of Greece and Rome and the glory of antiquity has soaked through our society also, descending through poets to ballad-mongers and from ballad-mongers to gutter-boys; and even to me. I may be regarded for the purpose here as the dunce of the school; but it was, in the medieval phrase, a grammar-school; and began with the Latin grammar.

Perhaps, however, the greatest name will be the best illustration. It was often said that Shakespeare is the typical Englishman in the fact that he had 'small Latin and less Greek". That is the only quality in which an average Eng-lishman like myself can claim to share. He had "small Latin and less Greek"; but he had plenty of Plutarch, and he was stuffed to bursting with the classical spirit. Consider, for instance, that he was of the Tudor time, which worshipped monarchy and was always saying, "There's such divinity doth hedge a king." And then consider what a revolution the mere reading of Plutarch in a translation could effect, in making the same man write:

> There was a Brutus once that would have brook'd
> The eternal devil to keep his state in Rome,
> As easily as a king.

But in a much deeper sense, Shakespeare was classical,

because he was civilized. Voltaire criticized him as a barbarian. But he was not a barbarian. The Germans have even admired him as a German; but by some strange accident of birth, he was not even a German. The point here, however, is that the classical spirit is no matter of names or allusions. I will take only one example to show what I mean by saying that Shakespeare was every bit as classical as Milton. Just before Othello kills his wife, he utters those words:

> If I quench thee, thou flaming minister,
> I can again the former light restore,
> Should I repent me; but once put out thy light,
> Thou cunning'st pattern of excelling nature,
> I know not where is that Promethean heat
> That can thy light relume.

Let me explain why I find it convenient to my argument to take this phrase as a type of the classical. Every classical phrase means much more than it says; in contrast with the too vivid and violent modern phrase, which says much more than it means. Whether it be romanticism in the nineteenth century, or realism in the twentieth century, its weakness is that it says so much more than it means. The phrase of Shakespeare, like the phrase of Virgil, is always much greater than its occasion. The cry of Othello goes far beyond the death of Desdemona; it goes far beyond death itself; it is a cry for life and the secret of life. Where is the beginning of that bewildering splendour by which we are; why can we not make life as we can make death? It may be worth remark in passing that even chemists who once claimed to manufacture everything, who could make synthetic leather or linen, have finally agreed that they cannot make synthetic life. They tell us that peculiar conditions must have existed once somewhere; though their laboratories should surely be capable of creating any conditions that could exist anywhere. "I know not where is that Promethean heat", nor do they. That cry still resounds unanswered in the universe. But the point for the present is that this profound resonance, striking such

echoes out of such hollows and abysses, could not be thus
achieved without a very deep understanding of classical
diction. It could not be done without the word "Promethean"; without the legend of Prometheus; without those
rolling polysyllables that are the power of Homer and Virgil.
In one practical and prosaic sense, of course, a man might
say what Othello says. He might say, "If I kill this woman,
how the devil am I to bring her to life again"; but hardly
with majesty; hardly with mystery; not precisely with all
those meanings and echoes of meanings which belong to a
great line of verse. But we need hardly condescend to deal
with the realistic critic; the serious gentleman who points out
the unquestionable fact that a man just about to smother his
wife with a pillow does not talk about Prometheus or specu-
late on the spiritual origin of life. It is enough to tell him, to
his bewilderment, that the soul never speaks until it speaks in
poetry; and that in our daily conversation we do not speak;
we only talk.

I have dwelt too long on that one example; but it happens
to be essential to the end of my argument to insist that Shakespeare did possess a certain great quality that is sometimes
denied to him, as well as many other great qualities, which
are generally conceded to him. Shakespeare did not merely
possess the things which Victor Hugo magnified and which
Voltaire mocked; wild imagination, wonderful lyric out-
bursts and the power of varying tragedy with the fantastic
and the grotesque. His work was more patchy than that of
pure classicists like Virgil or Racine, largely owing to the
accident of his own personal circumstances, mixed motives
and practical necessities. But the patchwork did not consist
only of purple patches. It did not consist only of passages that
are vivid in the romantic or unrestrained manner. He was
also capable of that structural dignity, and even of that
structural simplicity, in which we feel that we could rest
upon every word, as upon the stones of a stairway or a strong
bridge. It is also important to realize, in relation to the rest

of the thesis, that, after all, it was this classical part of
Shakespeare, much more than the romantic part of Shakespeare, that was handed on as a heritage to the English
poets immediately after him. His triumph was not followed
by a riot of fairies; but, on the contrary, by a return to
Hellenic gods or Hebraic archangels. By the soliloquies of
Satan and the choruses of *Samson Agonistes* Milton, in his
youth, exaggerated the youthful irresponsibility of Shakespeare; describing him merely as Fancy's child, who warbled
his native wood-notes wild. But Milton did not continue the
work, merely warbling wood-notes or behaving as fancifully
as a child of fancy. He set himself to do consistently and
consciously what Shakespeare had only done incidentally
and unconsciously; to bring English literature into the full
inheritance of Latin literature and the classical culture of
the Continent.

Dryden, the next great name after Milton, was in some
ways even more classical and certainly much more Continen-
tal. The whole tendency of his movement, which culminated
in Pope, was to make English poetry not only rational
enough to suit Boileau, but almost rational enough to soothe
Voltaire. The tendency had its deficiencies in other ways; but
that is not the point here. The point here is that with the
coming of the full eighteenth century, English literature is
entirely classical even in the merely scholarly sense of a study
of the classics. I summarize these things in a series, because
they illustrate the main truth of how long that Latin tradition retained its continuity; how steady was its progression;
and, above all, how very late, how very odd, and how very
temporary, was its interruption.

English–Latin literature and English–French literature
are much older than English literature. The Middle Ages
were international; and England was completely Continen-
tal. But even if we begin with Chaucer, who created English
by making it more than half French, the tradition of the
classics runs on steadily for fully five hundred years. The

last point at which it was undisputed might be represented by Macaulay. And he is an excellent example of my whole thesis. Macaulay had not, perhaps, a first-class mind; but he was completely in contact with the common mind. He was not one of our best writers, but he was emphatically one of our best-sellers. He was, above all, a popular writer; and he was popular because he was classical, in the sense that he took a classical education for granted. He identified England with a classical education and in one place he quotes a line from one of Milton's Latin poems in threatening an attack on what he would call the new cranks in Germany; "*Frangere Saxonicos Brittanno Marte phalanges*"; "To break the Saxon ranks with British battle." That phrase is a landmark, because it shows that not only Milton, but also Macaulay, thought of himself simply as British, and Saxon simply as German. England had not yet been taught that Englishmen were all Saxons, but under the name of Anglo-Saxons.

But while Macaulay was girding himself to attack the German cranks, there had already arisen in his own time and country a German crank who was not a German. His name was Thomas Carlyle; and he threw himself enthusiastically into a new racial theory that had come to England from Germany. It must be most carefully understood that it was a theory of race and not of nationality. The nations of Europe are now all under conditions that are recognized. Politically, each is independent of all the others. Culturally, each is connected with all the others. For all inherit the civilization of antiquity and of ancient Christendom. Germany, considered as one of the great European States, would be no proper subject for criticism here; but then Germany, considered as a great European State, is just as much a growth of the old civilization as the other European States. Classic antiquity was stamped all over it, whether we like the symbols or no; its eagle was the Roman eagle; its Kaiser was only the German for Caesar; even its Iron Cross was said to be of Christian origin. Its great medieval men were in full touch with the common culture, from Albertus Magnus to Albert Dürer. And it was, if possible, even more true in modern times than in medieval times. Goethe was, perhaps, the most purely classical sort of classicist who ever lived, and his watch was much more on the Mediterranean than on the Rhine. And Schiller called back from Hades the gods of Olympus and not the gods of Asgard.

What appeared in the North in the nineteenth century was an entirely new notion about race, as distinct from nationality. The new figure that appeared was not the German, but rather the Teuton. And a thing called the Teutonic race, afterwards called the Nordic race, and in moments of aberration, the Aryan race, was supposed to include the English as well as the Germans; at any rate by the Germans and by an increasing number of the English. The Nordic notion changed nineteenth-century England. All the educated English were taught something that none of the English had ever thought of in all their thousand years of history. It was an interpretation of history in general terms of race; it must not be confounded with the normal idea of nationality, or any sort of patriotism. No people were ever so passionately patriotic, not to say pigheadedly patriotic as the English of the eighteenth century, whose effective classes wrote, spoke, and almost thought in Latin and Greek, and lived by the culture of the Continent. The English were most English in the time when Johnson wrote all his epitaphs in Latin and Gibbon nearly wrote his great history in French. But this new nineteenth-century theory of race altered everything, at least in the most cultured class. A nation defends its boundaries, or it may want to extend its boundaries. A race has no boundaries; or at least it is impossible to prove that it has any boundaries. Norway, Sweden, Denmark, Germany, Austria, England, are entirely distinct as nations. But the tribal theory, that arose in Germany and spread to England, invoked Scandinavian as well as Saxon gods and talked as if the Anglo-Saxon race lived in Saxony. If the Teutonic tribalists of that time had wanted to annex Norfolk and Suffolk instead of Alsace and Lorraine, they would have had a better case on their own theories of language and ethnology. The very names of the North Folk and the South Folk would have shown that they in the great Teutonic folk's kultur "included were".

This modern or recent English cult of the Barbarian was a bad thing; for it is chiefly responsible for the international impression that the Englishman is a bad European. For by definition the Barbarian is a bad European. Now it is my chief aim here to insist that the Englishman can be and has now every intention of being a good European. And for that purpose, I have here insisted on three facts about this racial fad which reacted against the classic tradition of the Mediterranean. First, on how very late it was in our history; belonging to the time of my father, but not of my grandfather; and coming at the end of a thousand years of ever-accumulating classicism. Second, on how very superficial it was; even socially superficial, almost in the sense of snobbish. For, as I have already insisted, the Latin tradition is not a learned thing belonging to learned men; on the contrary, it is the common thing and the popular thing. In England, the classical past has penetrated into every cranny of common life, into the conversational speech and the very texture of society. Greek and Latin, as an influence, are not a luxury of any oligarchy. On the contrary, it was the reaction towards barbarism that was the mere affectation of an aristocracy. It was the tribal Teutonism that was a fashion for the fashionable. Professors who were academic and often aristocratic talked about Folklore; and duchesses organized Folk-Dances. But anybody might talk about heroic conduct, about platonic love, about a herculean effort, about a hectoring manner, about working for somebody like a trojan or bearing a toothache like a stoic. Any modern Englishman might speak of a forum for discussion or a quorum for an ordinary board-meeting of a company. But not many modern Englishmen, going to a committee, ever say to us gaily, "Let us go along to the Folk-moot." Few Anglo-Saxons trouble about whether the purest Anglo-Saxon requires them to talk about a waggon or a wain. But they all talk Latin when they want an omnibus.

It is often said by the very young that the Victorian Age, that is, the later nineteenth century in England, was a time of conventional virtue, a time of solid and stolid respectability. It was exactly the opposite. It was the one and only occasion on which the English went mad in favour of Barbarism. It was the one wild appearance of the Barbarian after a thousand years. From the time when the real Anglo-Saxon prayed in the Litany to be delivered *ab ira Normanorum*, from the fury of the Northmen, to the time when Lord Macaulay desired, as already noted, to break the Saxon ranks with a British attack like that of King Arthur, there had never been one single word said in all English literature in favour of the Barbarians against the grandeur of Rome. And the third thing about the barbaric interlude, on which I would insist most of all, is that it was ephemeral. It appeared in England very late and it disappeared from England very soon. Wild as it was while it lasted in the romances which were called the histories of Carlyle and Freeman and Froude, it never lasted long enough to disturb even the rather dismal externals of traditional life. . . . The barbaric fancy has been shed so rapidly precisely because it was not even a fancy of genuine barbarians but a fad of sophisticated snobs. It has gone quickly out of fashion, for the reason I have emphasized; that it never was anything except a fashion of the few; and the common people are full of the common heritage of Europe. What was once common may often have become vulgar; but in this sense even when it is vulgar it is still classical. The imagery and terminology of it are still classical. The Regius Professor at the University of Oxford wrote letters to *The Times* to prove that his very remote ancestors were moved entirely by the tragedy of Baldur; but meanwhile the grocer's assistant and the errand-boy in the

23

town of Oxford were still sending out vulgar Valentines covered with classical cupids; the last forlorn appearance of the little loves that lamented over the sparrow of Lesbia in the verses of Catullus. The nineteenth-century intellectuals went to the Wagner operas to watch Valkyrs and the Wotans of Nordic myth. But the cabman and the costermonger, who did not know a Valkyr from a Wagnerite, and to whom Götterdämmerung would only sound like a swear word, continued contentedly to go to the music-hall which is still named after the Muses.

I have, in a sense, made these suggestions pivot upon the name of Shakespeare, because he is, as I have said, in nothing more obviously the normal Englishman than in the fact that his whole culture was Greek and Latin, and yet he knew hardly any Latin or Greek. But he belonged to a time, and he inherited a history in which it was never counted conceivable that England should really be separate from Europe. No man has suffered more than Shakespeare from being quoted; and nothing normally is less Shakespearian than a quotation from Shakespeare. Thus the world has been bored with poor Juliet's casual and emotional exclamation: "What's in a name?", as if the poet who used words like "Hercules" and "Hecuba" as he did was ever so silly as to suppose that there was nothing in a name. In the same way, an extraordinary impression has been created that Shakespeare was entirely insular, merely by quoting about a line and a half out of a long passage in which he takes a very natural poetical pleasure in the fact that England is an island. It would be quite enough to quote the rest of the passage, to show that though Shakespeare liked England to be an island, he did not in the least like it to be an insular island. Everyone will know the tag I mean, the first lines, "This precious stone set in the silver sea, Which serves it in the office of a wall." He goes on to praise this fortress, but what does he praise it for? In what warfare is that fortress shown as famous and triumphant? Because it was the seat of princes:

> Renowned for their deeds as far from home,
> (For Christian service, and true chivalry,)
> As is the sepulchre in stubborn Jewry
> Of the world's ransom, blessed Mary's Son.

Why did Shakespeare think the English had been glorious? Because they had gone on the Crusades. Because they had ridden with Tancred the Italian and with Godfrey the Frank to the defence of a common Christian civilization. We have cast in our lot with civilization; and we shall not again forget what was found by Caesar and refounded by Augustine.

The Mind of the Middle Ages *v.* The Renaissance

It is beginning to be realized that the English are the eccentrics of the earth. They have produced an unusually large proportion of what they used to call Humourists and would not perhaps rather call Characters. And nothing is more curious about them than the contradiction of their consciousness and the unconsciousness of their own merits. It is nonsense, I regret to say, to claim that they are incapable of boasting. Sometimes they boast most magnificently of their weaknesses and deficiencies. Sometimes they boast of the more striking and outstanding virtues they do not possess. Sometimes they sink so low as to boast of not boasting. But it is perfectly true that they seem to be entirely unaware of the very existence of some of their most extraordinary claims to glory and distinction. One example among many is the fact that they have never realized the nature, let alone the scale, of the genius of Geoffrey Chaucer.

Most of the things that are hinted in depreciation of Chaucer could be said as easily in depreciation of Shakespeare. If Chaucer borrowed from Boccaccio and other writers, Shakespeare borrowed from anybody or anything, and often from the same French or Italian sources as his forerunner. The answer indeed is obvious and tremendous; that if Shakespeare borrowed, he jolly well paid back. . . . In the case of Shakespeare, as of Chaucer, his contemporaries and immediate successors seem to have been struck by something sweet or kindly about him, which they felt as too natural to be great in the grand style. He is chiefly praised, and occasionally rebuked, for freshness and spontaneity. Is it unfair to find a touch of that patronizing spirit even in the greatest among those who were less great?

26

> Or sweetest Shakespeare, fancy's child,
> Warble his native wood-notes wild.

I suspect Milton of meaning that his own organ-notes would be of a deeper and grander sort than wood-notes so innocently warbling. Yet somehow, as a summary of Shakespeare, the description does not strike one as comprehensive. Hung be the heavens with black . . . have lighted fools the way to dusty death . . . the multitudinous seas incarnadine . . . let the high gods, who keep this dreadful pother o'er our heads, find out their enemies now—these do not strike us exclusively as warblings.

The greatest poets of the world have a certain serenity, because they have not bothered to invent a small philosophy, but have rather inherited a large philosophy. It is, nine times out of ten, a philosophy which very great men share with very ordinary men. It is therefore not a theory which attracts attention as a theory. In these days, when Mr. Bernard Shaw is becoming gradually, amid general applause, the Grand Old Man of English Letters, it is perhaps ungracious to record that he did once say there was nobody, with the possible exception of Homer, whose intellect he despised so much as Shakespeare's. He has since said almost enough sensible things to outweigh even anything so silly as that. . . . Mr. Shaw had probably never read Homer; and there were passages in his Shakespearian criticism that might well raise a doubt about whether he ever read Shakespeare. But the point was that he could not, in all sincerity, see what the world saw in Homer and Shakespeare, because what the world saw was not what G.B.S. was then looking for. He was looking for that ghastly thing which Nonconformists call a Message, and continue to call a Message, even when they have become atheists and do not know who the Message is from. He was looking at a system; one of the very little systems that do very truly have their day. The system of Kant; the system of Hegel, the system of Schopenhauer and Nietzsche and Marx and all the rest. In each of these examples a man sprang up and pretended to have a thought that nobody had ever had. But the great poet only professes to express the thought that everybody has always had. The greatness of Homer does not consist in proving by the death of Hector, that the Will to Live is a delusion and a snare. It does not consist in proving, by the victory of Achilles, that the Will to Power must express itself in a Superman; for Achilles is not a Superman, but, on the contrary, a hero. The greatness of Homer consists in the fact that he could make men feel, what they were already quite ready to think, that life is a strange mystery in which a hero may err and another hero may fail. The poet makes men realize how great are the great emotions which they, in a smaller way, have already experienced. Every man who has tried to keep any good thing going, though it were a little club or paper or political protest, sounds the depths of his own soul when he hears the rolling line, which can only be rendered so feebly: "For truly in my heart and soul I know that Troy will fall." Every man who looks back on old days, for himself and others, and realizes the changes that vex something within us that is unchangeable, realizes better the immensity of his own meaning in the mere sound of the Greek words, which only mean, "For, as we have heard, you too, old man, were at one time happy." These words are in poetry, and therefore they have never been translated. But there are perhaps some people to whom even the words of Shakespeare need to be translated. Anyhow, what a man learns from *Romeo and Juliet* is not a new theory of sex; it is the mystery of something much more than what sensualists call sex, and what cads call sex appeal. What he learns from *Romeo and Juliet* is not to call first love "calf-love"; not to call even fleeting love a flirtation; but to understand that these things, which a million vulgarians have vulgarized are not vulgar. The great poet exists to show the small man how great he is. A man does not learn from Hamlet a new method of Psychoanalysis, or the proper treatment of lunatics. What he learns is not to despise the

soul as small; even when rather feminine critics say that
the will is weak. As if the will were ever strong enough for
the tasks that confront it in this world! The great poet is
alone strong enough to measure that broken strength we call
the weakness of man.

It has only been for a short time, a recent and disturbed
time of transition, that each writer has been expected to
write a new theory of all things, or draw a new wild map of
the world. The old writers were content to write of the old
world, but to write of it with an imaginative freshness which
made it in each case look like a new world. Before the time of
Shakespeare, men had grown used to the Ptolemaic astronomy, and since the time of Shakespeare men have grown
used to the Copernican astronomy. But poets have never
grown used to stars; and it is their business to prevent
anybody else ever growing used to them. And any man who
reads for the first time the words, "Night's candles are burnt
out", catches his breath and almost curses himself for having
neglected to look rightly, or sufficiently frequently, at the
grand and mysterious revolutions of night and day. Theories
soon grow stale; but things continue to be fresh. And, according to the ancient conception of his function, the poet was
concerned with things; with the tears of things, as in the
great lament of Virgil; with the delight in the number of
things, as in the light-hearted rhyme of Stevenson; with
thanks for things, as in the Franciscan Canticle of the Sun or
the *Benedicite Omnia Opera*. That behind those things there are
certain great truths is true; and those so unhappy as not to
believe in these truths may of course call them theories. But
the old poets did not consider that they had to compete and
bid against each other in the production of counter-theories.
The coming of the Christian cosmic conception made a vast
difference; the Christian poet had a more vivid hope than
the Pagan poet. Even when he was sometimes more stern, he
was always less sad. But, allowing for that more than human
change, the poets taught in a continuous tradition, and were

not in the least ashamed of being traditional. Each taught in an individual way; "with a perpetual slight novelty", as Aristotle said; but they were not a series of separate lunatics looking at separate worlds. One poet did not provide a pair of spectacles by which it appeared that the grass was blue, or another poet lecture on optics to teach people to say that the grass was orange; they both had the far harder and more heroic task of teaching people to feel that the grass is green. And because they continue their heroic task, the world, after every epoch of doubt and despair, always grows green again.

The life and death of Richard the Second constitute a tragedy which was perhaps the tragedy of English history, and was certainly the tragedy of English monarchy. It is seldom seen with any clearness; because of two prejudices that prevent men letting in on it the disinterested daylight of their minds. The first is the fact that, though it happened more than five hundred years ago, it is still dimly felt to be a Party Question. Shakespeare, in the time of the Tudors, saw it as an opportunity for exalting a sort of Divine Right; later writers, in the time of the Georges, have seen in it an opportunity for depreciating Divine Right. What is much more curious is the fact that neither ever noticed that the unfortunate Richard did not by any means merely stand for Divine Right; that in his earliest days he stood for what we are accustomed to consider much later rights, and for some which were, at least relatively speaking, the rights of democracy. The origin of this oblivion is in the second of the two modern prejudices. It is the extraordinary prejudice, sometimes identified with progress, to the effect that the world has always been growing more and more liberal, and that therefore there could be no popular ideals present in earlier times and forgotten in later times. The case of Richard the Second might have been specially staged in order to destroy this delusion. He was very far from being a faultless sovereign; he did various things which permit modern Parliamentarians to represent him as a despotic sovereign; but he was, by comparison with many contemporaries and most successors, a democratic sovereign. He did definitely attempt to help the democratic movement of his day, and he was definitely restrained from doing so. Shakespeare is full of sympathy for him, but Shakespeare was not full of sympathy for what most modern people would find sympathetic. He does not even mention the fact that the prince, whom he represents as bewailing the insult to his crown, and appealing to the sacred immunity of his chrism, had in his youth faced a rabble of roaring insurgent serfs, had declared that he himself would be their leader, the true demagogue of their new democracy, had promised to grant their demands, had disputed desperately with his nobles to get those demands granted, and had finally been overruled and forced to abandon the popular cause by that very baronial insolence which soon forced him to abandon the throne. If we ask why the greatest of dramatists was blind to the most dramatic of historic scenes, the young king claiming the leadership of the oppressed people, the explanation is perfectly simple. The explanation is that the whole theory, that "the thoughts of men are widen'd with the process of the suns," is all ignorant rubbish.

How could the suns widen anybody's thoughts? The explanation is that the men of Shakespeare's time understood far less of the democratic ideal than the men of Chaucer's time. The Tudors were occupied in their own time, as Shakespeare is occupied in his great play, with the sixteenth century mystical worship of the Prince. There was much more chance in the fourteenth century of having a mystical feeling about The People. Shakespeare's Richard is religious, to the extent of always calling himself The Lord's Anointed. The real Richard would also very probably have referred to the people as God's Flock. Ideas were mixed and misused in both periods, as in all periods; but in the time of Chaucer and Langland there was much more vague and general moral pressure upon the mind of the presence of problems of mere wealth and poverty, of the status of a peasant or the standards of a Christian, than there was in the time of Shakespeare and Spenser; of the splendour of Gloriana and the Imperial Votaress in the West. Therefore Shakespeare, great and human as he was, sees in Richard only the insulted king; and seems to think almost as little about the subjects of Richard as about the subjects of Lear.

But Richard had thought about the subjects of Richard. He had, in his early days and in his own way, tried to be a popular king in the sense of a popular leader. And though the popular ideas failed, and in some cases were bound to fail, they would have been much more present to the mind of a great writer of that time, than they were to the mind of one of the Queen's Servants under the last of the Tudors. In other words, even when there really is progress, as there certainly is growth, the progress is not a progress in everything, perfectly simple and universal and all of a piece. Civilizations go forward in some things, while they go backward in others. Men had better looms and steam hammers in 1850 than in 1750, but not handsomer hats and breeches or more dignified manners and oratory. And in the same way a man in the position of Shakespeare had more subtle and many-coloured arts, but not more simple and popular sympathies, than a man in the position of Langland. The Renaissance exalted the Poet, but even more it exalted the Prince; it was not primarily thinking about the Peasant. Therefore the greatest of all the great sons of the Renaissance, rolling out thousands of thunderous and intoxicant lines upon the single subject of the reign of King Richard the Second, does not trouble himself about The Peasants' War.

There is a type of student who has a curious subconscious itch in the presence of poetry; an itch for explaining it, in the hope of explaining it away. But this sort of critic is in any case unreliable, because, in dealing with a poem, he cannot distinguish between its occasion and its origin. He is the sort of commentator who, listening to the enchanted voice of Oberon, telling of mermaids and meteors and the purple

flower, is chiefly anxious to assure us that the imperial votaress was certainly Queen Elizabeth, and that there actually
was a pageant at Nobbin Castle, for a wedding in the Fitz-
nobbin family, in which a cupid and a mermaid figured in
such a manner as completely to explain William Shakespeare's remarks—and almost explain William Shakespeare.
It is all quite probable; it is all quite true; by all means, let us
be gravely grateful for the information. There were doubtless
a good many pageants and a good many parades of Cupid
and Dian; and I daresay a great many mermaids on a great
many dolphins' backs. But, by an odd chance, only one of
them ever, in the whole history of the world, uttered such
dulcet and harmonious breath that the rude sea grew civil at
her song, and certain stars shot madly from their spheres to
hear the sea-maid's music. That is the kind of thing that has
rather a way of only happening once. And if we really must
find out where it came from, or why it came, we shall be wise
to guess that it had a good deal less to do with the Mermaid
at Nobbin Castle than with that other Mermaid at which
Mr. William Shakespeare of Stratford sometimes took a
little more wine than was good for him.

Chaucer was not an unsuccessful man. For the greater
part of his life he was a successful man and a poet; and yet
we cannot say exactly that he was a successful poet. That is,
he was not successful as a poet in the way in which some of
his contemporaries were successful as poets; praised and
applauded as poets; crowned and enthroned as poets. In
this respect there is a curious parallel between the mystery
of Chaucer and the mystery of Shakespeare. They were
neither of them failures or outcasts; they both seem to have
had a good deal of solid success, though Shakespeare was
wealthiest in later life and Chaucer in middle life. But they
were more successful than famous; and more famous than
glorious. The odd obscurity of Shakespeare, in some aspects,
which has been the negative opportunity of so many cranks
and quacks, is a real fact so far as it goes, and it can best be

measured if we compare it, for instance, with the flamboyant fame of Ronsard a few years before in France. Some say that Shakespeare's death was disreputable; it is a far more creepy and uncanny fact that his life was respectable. He lived and died, not like a first-rate failure, but like a fourth-rate success. He lived and died a proper provincial burgess, a few years after Ronsard had gathered round his gorgeous death-bed that great assembly of nobles and princes in the robes of religion, and proclaimed to all Europe as with a trumpet that no man born had known so much glory as he, and that he was weary of it and thirsty for the glory of God. The obscure death of Shakespeare is almost as startling a contrast, whether it was disreputable or respectable.

I know that commentators, or those critics who chiefly shine as commentators, are often gravely anxious to clear great men of the charge of talking nonsense. They apply it to Shakespeare; who has whole passages in which he talks nothing but nonsense. When Hamlet says, "I am but mad north-north-west: when the wind is southerly, I know a hawk from a hand-saw," the remark strikes his critics as one eminently suitable for scientific and rationalizing treatment; some hastily amending it to, "I know a hawk from a heron-shaw," and the other, I think, inventing some new tool or utensil called a hawk. I know nothing of these things; they may be right. But seeing that the man was a fantastic humor-ist in any case, and pretending to be a lunatic at that, and seeing he starts the very same sentence by saying he is mad, it seems to me, as a humble fellow-habitant of Hanwell, that he probably meant to say, "a hawk from a hand-saw", as he might have said, "a bishop from a blunderbuss" or, "a postman from a pickle-jar". . . . There is something a little sinister in the number of mad people there are in Shakespeare. We say that he uses his fools to brighten the dark back-ground of tragedy; I think he sometimes uses them to darken it. Somewhere on that highest of all human towers there is a tile loose. There is something that rattles rather crazily in the high wind of the highest of mortal tragedies. What is felt faintly even in Shakespeare is felt far more intensely in the other Elizabethan and Jacobean dramatists; they seem to go in for dancing ballets of lunatics and choruses of idiots, until sanity is the exception rather than the rule. In some ways Chaucer's age was even harsher than Shakespeare's, but even its ferocity was rational. ... In other words, the medieval mind did not really believe that the truth was to be found by going to extremes. And the Elizabethan mind had already had a sort of hint that it might be found there; at the extreme edges of existence and precipices of the human imagination.

Everything, even the great poetry of Elizabethan times, was a little too much involved. In literature it was the age of conceits. In politics it was the age of conspiracies. In those conspiracies there is a curious absence of the fresh popular spirit that often blew like a wind even through the heresies and horrors of the Middle Ages. None of it was in the same world with the Peasants' Rising. The age of Richard the Second was an age of revolutions. The age of Elizabeth was an age of plots. And we all know that this was mirrored more or less even in the mightiest minds of that epoch. It is almost in a double sense that we talk about Shakespeare's "plots". In almost every case, it is a plot about a plot. He has even a sort of restlessness vaguely connected with the sixteenth-century sense of the importance and the insecurity of princes. "Uneasy lies the head that wears a crown"; and also the head that has crowns on the brain.

That Shakespeare is the English giant, all but alone in his stature among the sons of men, is a truth that does not really diminish with distance. But it is a truth with two aspects; a shield with two sides; a sword with two edges. It is exactly because Shakespeare is an English giant that he blocks up the perspective of English history. He is as disproportionate to his own age as to every age; but he throws a misleading lime-light on his own age and throws a gigantic shadow back on the other ages. For this reason many will not even know what I mean, when I talk about the greater spaciousness around the medieval poet. If the matter were pushed to a challenge, however, I could perhaps illustrate my meaning even better with another medieval poet. It is vaguely implied that Shakespeare was always jolly and Dante always gloomy. But, in a philosophical sense, it is almost the other way. It is notably so, if, so to speak, we actually bring Shakespeare to the test of Dante. Do we not know in our hearts that Shakespeare could have dealt with Dante's Hell but hardly with Dante's Heaven? In so far as it is possible to be greater than anything that is really great, the man who wrote of Romeo and Juliet might have made something even more poignant out of Paolo and Francesca. The man who uttered that pulverizing "He has no children", over the butchery in the house of Macduff, might have picked out yet more awful and telling words for the father's cry out of the Tower of Hunger. But the Tower of Hunger is not spacious. And when Dante is really dealing with the dance of the liberated virtues in the vasty heights of heaven, he is spacious. He is spacious when he talks of Liberty; he is spacious when he talks of Love. It is so in the famous words at the end about Love driving the sun and stars; it is the same in the far less famous and far finer passage, in which he hails the huge magnanimity of God in giving to the human spirit the one gift worth having; which is Liberty. Nobody but a fool will say that Shakespeare was a pessimist; but we may, in this limited sense, say that he was a pagan; in so far that he is at his greatest in describing great spirits in chains. In that sense, his most serious plays are an Inferno. Anyhow, they are certainly not a Paradiso.

I only use Shakespeare here as a parallel, and I will not continue it indefinitely as a parenthesis. Otherwise I should, of course, qualify the word paganism by well-known facts about his life, as well as by the whole tone of his literature. That Shakespeare was a Catholic is a thing that every Catholic feels by every sort of convergent common sense to be true. It is supported by the few external and political facts we know; it is utterly unmistakable in the general spirit and atmosphere; and in nothing more than in the scepticism, which appears in some aspects to be paganism. But I am not talking about the various kinds of Catholic; I am talking about the atmosphere of the sixteenth century as compared with the fourteenth century. And I say that while the former was more refined, it was in certain special ways more restricted, or properly speaking, more concentrated. Shakespeare is more concentrated on Hamlet than Dante is upon Hell; for the very reason that Dante's mind is full of the larger plan of which this is merely a part.

This chapter consists of passages from Chesterton's book *Chaucer* published by Faber & Faber, by whose kind permission the extracts are included.

Part Two: The Tragedies

The True Hamlet

A recent critic enunciates a view of Hamlet which flies flat in
the face of every accepted theory; he maintains that Hamlet
was not irresolute, not over-intellectual, not procrastinating,
not weak. The challenge, erroneous as it may be, is spirited,
ingenious and well-reasoned, and it can do nothing but
honour to Shakespeare. The more varied are the versions of
friends and enemies, the more flatly irreconcilable are the
opinions of various men about Hamlet, the more he resembles
a real man. The characters of fiction, mysterious as they are,
are far less mysterious than the figures of history. Men have
agreed about Hamlet vastly more than they have agreed
about Caesar or Mahomet or Cromwell or Mr. Gladstone
or Cecil Rhodes. Nobody supposes that Mr. Gladstone
was a solar myth; nobody has started the theory that Mr.
Rhodes is only the hideous phantom of an idle dream. Yet
hardly three men agree about either of them, hardly anyone
knows that some new and suggestive view of them might not
be started at any moment. If Hamlet can be thus surprised,
if he can be thus taken in the rear, it is a great tribute to the
solidity of the figure. If from another standpoint he appears
like another statue, it shows at least that the figure is made of
marble and not of cardboard. Neither the man who thinks
Lord Beaconsfield a hero nor the man who thinks him a snob
doubts his existence. It is a great tribute to literature if
neither the man who thinks Hamlet a weakling, nor the man
who thinks him a hero ever thinks of doubting Hamlet's
existence.

Personally, I think the critic absolutely right in denouncing
the idea that Hamlet was a "witty weakling". There is a
great difference between a weakness which is at liberty and

a strength which is rusted and clogged. Hamlet was not a weak man fundamentally. Shakespeare never forgets to remind us that he had an elemental force and fire in him, liable to burst out and strike everyone with terror.

> "Yet have I something in me dangerous
> Which let thy wisdom fear."

But Hamlet was a man in whom the faculty of action had been clogged, not by the smallness of his moral nature, but by the greatness of his intellectual. Actions were really important to him, only they were not quite so dazzling and dramatic as thoughts. He belonged to a type of man which some men will never understand, the man for whom what happens inside his head does actually and literally happen; for whom ideas are adventures, for whom metaphors are living monsters, for whom an intellectual parallel has the irrevocable sanctity of a marriage ceremony. Hamlet failed, but through the greatness of his upper, not the weakness of his lower, storey. He was a giant, but he was top-heavy.

But while I warmly agree in holding that the moral greatness of Hamlet is enormously underrated, I cannot agree that Hamlet was a moral success. If this is true, indeed, the whole story loses its central meaning; if the hero was a success, the play is a failure. Surely no one who remembers Hamlet's tremendous speech, beginning:

> "O what a rogue and peasant slave am I,"

can share the critic's conclusion:

> "He is not here condemning himself for inaction, there
> is no cause for the reproach, he is using the resources
> of passion and eloquence to spur himself to action."

It is difficult for me to imagine anyone reading that appalling cry out of the very hell of inutility and think that Hamlet is not condemning himself for inaction. Hamlet may, of course, be only casually mentioning that he is a moral coward; for the matter of that, the Ghost may be only cracking a joke when he says he has been murdered. But if ever there was sincerity in any human utterance, there is in the remorse of Hamlet.

The truth is that Shakespeare's Hamlet is immeasurably vaster than any mere ethical denunciation or ethical defence. Figures like this, scribbled in a few pages of pen and ink, can claim, like living human beings, to be judged by Omniscience. To call Hamlet a "witty weakling" is entirely to miss the point, which is his greatness; to call him a triumphant hero is to miss a point quite as profound. It is the business of art to seize these nameless points of greatness and littleness; the truth is not so much that art is immoral as that art has to single out sins that are not to be found in any decalogue and virtues that cannot be named in any allegory. But upon the whole it is always more indulgent than philanthropy. Falstaff was neither brave nor honest, nor chaste, nor temperate, nor clean, but he had the eighth cardinal virtue for which no name has ever been found. Hamlet was not fitted for this world; but Shakespeare does not dare to say whether he was too good or too bad for it.

Hamlet and the Psycho-analyst

This morning, for a long stretch of hours before breakfast, and even as it were merging into breakfast, and almost overlapping breakfast, I was engaged in scientific researches in the great new department of psycho-analysis. Every journalist knows by this time that psycho-analysis largely depends on the study of dreams. But in order to study our dreams it is necessary to dream; and in order to dream it is necessary to sleep. So, while others threw away the golden hours in lighter and less learned occupations, while ignorant and superstitious peasants were already digging in their ignorant and superstitious kitchen-gardens, to produce their ignorant and superstitious beans and potatoes, while priests were performing their pious mummeries and poets composing lyrics on listening to the skylark—I myself was pioneering hundreds of years ahead of this benighted century; ruthlessly and progressively probing into all the various horrible nightmares, from which a happier future will take its oracles and its commandments. I will not describe my dreams in detail; I am not quite so ruthless a psychologist as all that. And indeed it strikes me as possible that the new psychologist will be rather a bore at breakfast. My dream was something about wandering in some sort of catacombs under the Albert Hall, and it involved eating jumbles (a brown flexible cake now almost gone from us, like so many glories of England) and also arguing with a Theosophist. I cannot fit this in very well with Freud and his theory of suppressed impulses. For I swear I never in my life suppressed the impulse to eat a jumble or to argue with a Theosophist. And as for wandering about in the Albert Hall, nobody could ever have had an impulse to do that.

When I came down to breakfast I looked at the morning paper; not (as you humorously suggest) at the evening paper. I had not pursued my scientific studies quite so earnestly as that. I looked at the morning paper, as I say, and found it contained a good deal about psycho-analysis; indeed it explained almost everything about psycho-analysis except what it was. This was naturally a thing which newspapers would present in a rather fragmentary fashion; and I fitted the fragments together as best I could. Apparently the dreams were merely symbols; and apparently symbols of something very savage and horrible which remained a secret. This seems to me a highly unscientific use of the word symbol. A symbol is not a disguise but rather a display; the best expression of something that cannot otherwise be expressed. Eating a jumble may mean that I wished to bite off my father's nose (the mother-complex being strong in me); but it does not seem to show much symbolic talent. The Albert Hall may imply the murder of an uncle; but it hardly makes itself very clear. And we do not seem to be getting much nearer the truth by dreaming, if we hide things by night more completely than we repress them by day. Anyhow, the murdered uncle reminds me of Hamlet, of whom more anon; at the moment I am merely remarking that my newspaper was a little vague; and I was all the more relieved to open my *London Mercury* and find an article on the subject by so able and suggestive a writer as Mr. J. D. Beresford, who practically asked himself whether he should become a psycho-analyst or continue to be a novelist. It will readily be understood that he did not put it precisely in these words; he would probably put psycho-analysis higher, and very possibly his own fiction lower; for men of genius are often innocent enough of their own genuine originality. That is a form of the unconscious mind with which none of us will quarrel. But I have no desire to watch a man of genius tying himself in knots and perhaps dying in agony, in the attempt to be conscious of his own unconsciousness. I have seen too many unfortunate sceptics thus committing suicide by self-contradiction. Haeckel and his Determinists, in my youth, bullied us all about the urgent necessity of choosing a philosophy which would prove the impossibility of choosing anything. No doubt the new psychology will somehow enable us to know what we are doing, about all that we do without knowing it. These things come and go and pass through their phases in order, from the time when they are as experimental as Freudianism to the time when they are as exploded as Darwinism. But I never can understand men allowing things so visibly fugitive to hide things that are visibly permanent, like morals and religion and (what is in question here) the art of letters. *Ars longa, scientia brevis.*

Anyhow, as has been said, psycho-analysis depends in practice upon the interpretation of dreams. I do not know whether making masses of people, chiefly children, confess their dreams, would lead to a great output of literature; though it would certainly lead, if I know anything of human nature, to a glorious output of lies. There is something touching in the inhuman innocence of the psychologist who is already talking of the scientific exactitude of results reached by the one particular sort of evidence that cannot conceivably be checked or tested in any way whatever. But the general notion of finding signs in dreams is as old as the world; but even the special theory of it is older than many seem to suppose. Indeed, it is not only old but obvious; and was never discovered, because it was always noticed. Long before the present fashion I myself (who, heaven knows, am no psychologist) remember saying that as there is truth in all popular traditions, there is truth in the popular saying that dreams go by the rule of contraries. That is, that a man does often think at night about the very things he does not think by day. But the popular saying had in it a certain virtue never found in the anti-popular sciences of our day. Popular superstition has one enormous element of sanity; it is never serious. We talk of ages like the medieval as the ages of faith;

46

but it would be quite as true a tribute to call them the ages of doubt; of a healthy doubt and even a healthy derision. there was always something more or less consciously grotesque about an old ghost story. There was fun mixed with the fear; and the yokels knew too much about turnips not occasionally to think of turnip-ghosts. There is no fun about psycho-analysis. One yokel would say, "Ar, they do say dreams go by contraries." And then the others would say, "Ar," and they would all laugh in a deep internal fashion. But when the critic says that Freud's theory is among scientific theories the most attractive for novelists, "it was the theory of sex, the all but universal theme of the novel," it is clear that our audience is slower and more solemn than the yokels. For nobody laughs at all. People seem to have lost the power of reacting to the humorous stimulus. When one milkmaid dreamed of a funeral, the other milkmaid said, "That means a wedding," and then they would both giggle. But when Mr. Beresford says that the theory "adumbrated the suggestion of a freer morality, by dwelling upon the physical and spiritual necessity for the liberation of impulse," the point seems somehow to be missed. Not a single giggle is heard in the deep and disappointing silence. It seems truly strange that when a modern and brilliant artist actually provides jokes far more truly humorous than the rude jests of the yokels and the milkmaids, the finer effort should meet with the feebler response. It is but an example of the unnatural solemnity, like an artificial vacuum in which all these modern experiments are conducted. But no doubt if Freud had enjoyed the opportunity of explaining his ideas in an ancient ale-house, they would have met with more spontaneous applause.

Mr. Beresford must therefore excuse me if, with a sincere desire to follow his serious argument seriously, I note at the beginning a certain normal element of comedy of which critics of his school seem to be rather unconscious. When they ask whether this theory of the nemesis of suppression can

serve the purposes of great literary work, it would seem
natural at first to test it by the example of the greatest literary
works. And judged by this scientific test, it must be admitted
that our literary classics would appear to fail. Lady Macbeth
does not suffer as a sleep-walker because she has resisted the
impulse to murder Duncan, but rather (by some curious
trick of thought) because she has yielded to it. Hamlet's
uncle is in a morbid frame of mind, not as one would
naturally expect because he had thwarted his own development by leaving his own brother alive and in possession, but
actually because he has triumphantly liberated himself from
the morbid impulse to pour poison in his brother's ear.
On the theory of psycho-analysis as expounded, a man ought
to be haunted by the ghosts of all the men he has not
murdered. Even if they were limited to those he has felt a
vague fancy for murdering, they might make a respectable
crowd to follow at his heels. Yet Shakespeare certainly seems
to represent Macbeth as haunted by Banquo, whom he
removed at one blow from the light of the sun and from his
own sub-consciousness. Hell ought to mean the regret for lost
opportunities for crime; the insupportable thought of
houses still standing unburned or unburgled, or of wealthy
uncles still walking about alive with their projecting watch-
chains. Yet Dante certainly seemed to represent it as concerned exclusively with things done and done with, and not
as merely the morbidly congested imagination of a thief
who had not thieved and a murderer who had not murdered.
In short, it is only too apparent that the poets and sages of the
past knew very little of psycho-analysis and managed to
achieve their literary effects without it.

This is but a preliminary point and I touch the more
serious problem in a few minutes. For the moment I only
take the test of literary experience, and of how independent
of such theories have been the real masterpieces of man.
Men are still excited over the poetic parts of poets like
Shakespeare and Dante; if they go to sleep it is over the

48

scientific parts. It is over some system of the spheres which Dante thought the very latest astronomy, or some argument about the humours of the body which Shakespeare thought the very latest physiology. But there is one incidental moral in the matter that seems to me topical and rather arresting. It concerns the idea of punishment. The psycho-analysts continue to buzz in a mysterious manner round the problem of Hamlet. They are especially interested in the things of which Hamlet was unconscious, not to mention the things of which Shakespeare was unconscious. It is in vain for old-fashioned rationalists like myself to point out that this is like dissecting the brain of Puck or revealing the real private life of Punch and Judy. The discussion no longer revolves round whether Hamlet is mad, but whether everybody is mad, especially the experts investigating the madness. And the curious thing about this process is that even when the critics are really subtle enough to see subtle things, they are never simple enough to see self-evident things. A really fine critic is reported as arguing that in Hamlet the consciousness willed one thing and the subconsciousness another. Apparently the conscious Hamlet had unreservedly embraced and even welcomed the obligation of vengeance, but the shock (we are told) had rendered the whole subject painful and started a strange and secret aversion to the scheme. It did not seem to occur to the writers that there might possibly be something slightly painful, at the best, in cutting the throat of your own uncle and the husband of your own mother. There might certainly be an aversion from the act; but I do not quite see why it should be an unconscious aversion. It seems just possible that a man might be quite conscious of not liking such a job. Where he differed from the modern morality was that he believed in the possibility of disliking it and yet doing it.

But to follow the argument of these critics one would think that murdering the head of one's family was a sort of family festivity or family joke; a gay and innocent indulgence into which the young prince would naturally have thrown himself with thoughtless exuberance, were it not for the dark and secretive thoughts that had given him an unaccountable distaste for it. Suppose it were borne in upon one of these modern middle-class critics of my own rank and routine of life (possibly through his confidence in the messages at a Spiritualist séance) that it was his business to go home to Brompton or Surbiton and stick the carving-knife into Uncle William, who had poisoned somebody and was beyond the reach of the law. It is possible that the critic's first thought would be that it was a happy way of spending a half-holiday; and that only in the critic's subconsciousness the suspicion would stir that there was something unhappy about the whole business. But it seems also possible that the regret might not be confined to his subconsciousness but might swim almost to the surface of his consciousness. In plain words, this sort of criticism has lost the last rags of common sense. Hamlet requires no such subconscious explanation, for he explains himself and was perhaps rather too fond of doing so. He was a man to whom duty had come in a very dreadful and repulsive form and to a man not fitted for that form of duty. There was a conflict, but he was conscious of it from beginning to end. He was not an unconscious person but a far too conscious one.

Strangely enough this theory of subconscious repulsion in the dramatic character is itself an example of subconscious repulsion in the modern critic. It is the critic who has a sort of subliminal prejudice which makes him avoid something that seems very simple to others. The thing which he secretly and obscurely avoids from the start is the very simple fact of the morality in which Shakespeare did believe, as distinct from all the crude psychology in which he almost certainly did not believe. Shakespeare certainly did believe in the struggle between duty and inclination. The critic instinctively avoids the admission that Hamlet's was a struggle between duty and inclination and tries to substitute a struggle between consciousness and subconsciousness. He gives Hamlet a complex to avoid giving him a conscience. But he is actually forced to talk as if it was a man's natural inclination to kill an uncle, because he does not want to admit that it might be his duty to kill him. He is really driven to talking as if some dark and secretive monomania alone prevents us all from killing our uncles. He is driven to this because he will not even take seriously the simple and, if you will, primitive morality upon which the tragedy is built. For that morality involves three moral propositions, from which the whole of the morbid modern subconsciousness does really recoil as from an ugly jar of pain. These principles are: first, that it may be our main business to do the right thing, even when we detest doing it; second, that the right thing may involve punishing some person, especially some powerful person; third, that the just process of punishment may take the form of fighting and killing. The modern critic is prejudiced against the first principle and calls it asceticism; he is prejudiced against the second principle and calls it vindictiveness; he is prejudiced against the third and generally calls it militarism. That it actually might be the duty of a young man to risk his own life, much against his own inclination, by drawing a sword and killing a tyrant, that is an idea instinctively avoided by this particular mood of modern times. That is why tyrants have such a good time in modern times. And in order to avoid this plain and obvious meaning of war as a duty and peace as a temptation, the critic has to turn the whole play upside down, and seek its meaning in modern notions so remote as to be in this connection meaningless. He has to make William Shakespeare of Stratford one of the pupils of Professor Freud. He has to make him a champion of psycho-analysis; he has to fit Hamlet's soul somehow into the classifications of Freud and Jung. He has to interpret the whole thing by a new morality that Shakespeare had never heard of, because he has an intense internal dislike of the old morality that

Shakespeare could not help hearing of. And that morality, which some of us believe to be based on a much more realistic psychology, is that punishment as punishment is a perfectly healthy process, not merely because it is reform, but also because it is expiation. What the modern world means by proposing to substitute pity for punishment is really very simple. It is that the modern world dare not punish those who are punishable but only those who are pitiable. It would never touch anyone so important as King Claudius or Kaiser William.

Now this truth is highly topical just now. The point about Hamlet was that he wavered, very excusably, in something that had to be done; and this is the point quite apart from whether we ourselves would have done it. That was pointed out long ago by Browning in *The Statue and the Bust*. He argued that even if the motive for acting was bad, the motive for not acting was worse. And an action or inaction is judged by its real motive not by whether somebody else might have done the same thing from a better motive. Whether or no the tyrannicide of Hamlet was a duty, it was accepted as a duty and it was shirked as a duty. And that is precisely true of a tyrannicide like that for which everybody clamoured at the conclusion of the Great War. It may have been right or wrong to punish the Kaiser; it was certainly no more right to punish the German generals and admirals for their atrocities. But even if it was wrong, it was not abandoned because it was wrong. It was abandoned for all those motives —weakness and mutability of mood which we associate with the name of Hamlet. It might be glory or ignominy to shed the blood of imperial enemies, but it is certainly ignominy to shout for what you dare not shed; "to fall a-cursing like a common drab, a scullion". Granted that we had no better motives than we had then or have now, it would certainly have been more dignified if we had fatted all the region-kites with this slave's offal. The motive is the only moral test. A saint might provide us with a higher motive for forgiving the War-Lords who butchered Fryatt and Edith Cavell. But

we have not forgiven the War-Lords. We have simply forgotten the War. We have not pardoned like Christ; we have
only procrastinated like Hamlet. Our highest motive has
been laziness; our commonest motive has been money. In this
respect indeed I must apologize to the charming and chival-
rous Prince of Denmark for comparing him, even on a single
point, with the princes of finance and the professional politicians of our time. At least Hamlet did not spare Claudius
solely because he hoped to get money out of him for the
salaries of the Players, or meant to do a deal with him about
wine supplied to Elsinore or debts contracted at Wittenburg.
Still less was Hamlet acting entirely in the interests of Shylock, an inhabitant of the distant city of Venice. Doubtless
Hamlet was sent to England in order that he might develop
further these higher motives for peace and pardon. " 'Twill
not be noticed in him there; there the men are as mad as he."
  It is therefore very natural that men should be trying to
dissolve the moral problem of Hamlet into the unmoral
elements of consciousness and unconsciousness. The sort of
duty that Hamlet shirked is exactly the sort of duty that we
are all shirking, that of dethroning justice and vindicating
truth. Many are now in a mood to deny that it is a duty
because it is a danger. This applies, of course, not only to
international but internal and especially industrial matters.
Capitalism was allowed to grow into a towering tyranny in
England because the English were always putting off their
popular revolution, just as the Prince of Denmark put off his
palace revolution. They lectured the French about their
love of bloody revolutions, exactly as they are now lecturing
the French about their love of bloody wars. But the patience
which suffered England to be turned into a plutocracy was
not the patience of the saints; it was that patience which
paralysed the noble prince of the tragedy; *accidia* and the
great refusal. In any case, the vital point is that by refusing to
punish the powerful we soon lost the very idea of punishment
and turned our police into a mere persecution of the poor.

53

King Claudius: Dominus Rex

I once very nearly wrote a fairy tale on the old theme of a country where all wishes come true; and where, as a matter of fact, everybody maintained a terrified silence, being afraid to mention anything for fear it should happen. Not only their fancies, but their figures of speech would instantly materialize; so that, if a man inadvertently observed, "I must have lost my head," his head instantly rolled away like a cannonball; or if he said, "I'm rather up a tree just now," he was borne aloft by a sprouting palm or pine that sprang up immediately under him. The result was that everybody felt a little nervous; as I sometimes think most of us would feel in most of the Utopias and ideal social states. But I am beginning to feel a little nervous now; because I rather fancy we must be living in a fairy-land of this kind. The world is growing so wild and experimental that almost everything that can be suggested as a fancy is found to be already a fact.

Now, I am far from suggesting that the experiment of acting *Hamlet* in modern costume is quite so quaint a conception as any of these. Doubtless there is a great deal to be said for it. . . . I remember saying a long time ago that, as a matter of fact, this is the only period of human history when it would have seemed particularly incongruous or inconceivable to act a heroic scene in the costume of the period. People use this argument and say, "Shakespeare thought of Hamlet as a sixteenth-century gentleman; Garrick acted Hamlet as an eighteenth-century gentleman; why cannot we present him as a twentieth-century gentleman?" The obvious answer is "Why indeed?" Why do we feel the costume of our period to be unsuitable? The very question proves that we *do* feel it to be unsuitable. There must be

54

some reason for our feeling so different from the feeling of our fathers. Is it conceivable that there may be something a little unsuitable to the soul of man about the costume? Or about the period?

I think the answer is that to dress Hamlet up in the second-hand clothes of the Manchester merchant of the nineteenth century is not to free him, but to restrain him. And what we call modern costume is simply the last patchwork compromise of the hideous black commercial uniform that the Victorians thought correct and conventional. A man is much freer in an inky cloak than he is in an inky coat. And when the Victorian merchants wore customary suits of solemn black, they were not confined to one individual, to one tragic prince rather ostentatiously in mourning. They really were customary suits; and no bank clerk was allowed to go to business in anything else. What we call modern costume is simply the remains of that queer Puritanical convention; and to make Hamlet modern is not in the least to make him more unconventional. It is to make him more conventional. But I feel this to be even more true in the case of the King, the villain of the story. A dramatic critic for whom I have a very high regard indeed declares that King Claudius becomes much more vivid and human in modern costume. In one sense this may be true, but not in the sense in which I have always understood the character of that agreeable gentleman. The point interests me a little because (to reveal a dark episode in my life) I did once, in one sense, act King Claudius in modern costume. It was, indeed, in a very mild reading of *Hamlet*; but even there I felt that the modern setting made the reading far too mild. It was in my own house, and I became painfully conscious of all the respects in which that lowly cot differs from the Castle of Elsinore.

Whatever else King Claudius was, it struck me at the time that he was a very noisy gentleman. He was very fond of noise; apparently, like a true artist, of noise for noise's sake. Again and again there is mention of his taste for having his smallest domestic actions saluted with a blare of trumpets and a roar of guns. He himself declares it in glorious blank verse that thunders like the guns and trumpets. Hamlet mentions it, in a passage of imperfect sympathy, which has sometimes given me a horrible feeling that Hamlet had a hankering after temperance. Anyhow the King's toasts at table and similar things were always saluted in this stupendous and crashing style. And I felt considerable sympathy and even envy. I wish that, whenever I happen to drink a glass of wine, a small park of artillery in the back garden could be timed to explode and the echoes roll back respeaking earthly thunder. I wish there were a brass band, with cannons in the orchestra in the Russian manner, to punctuate any little social observation I might have to make, such as "Shall we join the ladies?" or "Take another cigar." That was the way King Claudius went through life; and I do seriously think it throws, and was meant to throw, a great deal of light on his character.

I think Claudius is a very fine and true study of the Usurper; because he is the man who really wants to be King. A man must take the monarchy very seriously to be a Usurper. In a certain somewhat irregular sense, he must be an extreme Royalist. And in the sixteenth century especially the Crown was really a sort of dizzy and divine glory; like having stolen the sun out of the sky. That I think is the meaning of all the towering pomp of trumpet and cannon with which this Usurper surrounds himself; he is enjoying what he has stolen. He has not stolen mere money; he is not enjoying mere land; what he is enjoying is being *Dominus Rex*. And that explains, what nobody else ever really explains, why Shakespeare has put into the mouth of this low impostor and assassin the most stately declaration of the doctrine of the Divine Right of Kings. That is why he says, "There's such divinity doth hedge a king." That is why in facing the fury of Laertes, he can play the man, because he can play the King. The liar fights bravely for his lie. The dream of royalty he has raised around him has become a sort of reality. It is for this that he lives; and for this, in the queer inversion of human virtue, he will almost die. Perhaps it was something hypnotic and overpowering in his haughty pose that drove Hamlet to such raging recriminations about his pettiness and baseness, comparing him to a pickpocket and a slave.

Now my conception of Claudius may be right or wrong, but, anyhow, it is a character Shakespeare might well have drawn. But it is a character that no man in modern clothes could really represent. We do not fire off cannons when we drink a glass of claret any more than we wear crowns when we are kings, or swords when we are gentlemen. The whole of that superb self-expression of the Usurper in pomp and noise becomes impossible. The fulfilment of the false king's dream cannot even be suggested in modern scenery. It may have many morals; but the moral that strikes me is that of the extreme narrowness of the modern world.

The Orthodoxy of Hamlet

I am sometimes tempted to think (like every other person who does think) that the people would always be right if only they were not educated. But this is, of course, quite the wrong way of putting it. The truth is that there is no such thing as education; there is only this education and that education. We are all ready to die in order to give the people this education, and (I hope sincerely) we are all ready to die to prevent the people having that education. Dr. Strong, in *David Copperfield*, educated little boys; but Mr. Fagin in *Oliver Twist*, also educated little boys; they were both what we now call 'educationalists'.

But though the first mode of statement is certainly erroneous, one is driven back upon it sometimes in considering the case of the drama. I enjoy the drama far too much ever to be a dramatic critic; and I think that in this I am at one with that real people which never speaks. If anybody wants to know what political democracy is, the answer is simple; it is a desperate and partly hopeless attempt to get at the opinion of the best people—that is, of the people who do not trust themselves. A man can rise to any rank in an oligarchy. But an oligarchy is simply a prize for impudence. An oligarchy says that the victor may be any kind of man, so long as he is not a humble man.

A man in an oligarchical state (such as our own) may become famous by having money, or famous by having an eye for colour, or famous for having social or financial or military success. But he cannot become famous for having humility, like the great saints. Consequently all the simple and hesitating human people are kept entirely out of the running; and the cads stand for the common people, although as a matter of fact the cads are a minority of the common people. So it is quite especially with the drama. It is utterly untrue that the people do not like Shakespeare. That part of the people that does not like Shakespeare is simply that part of the people that is depopularized. If a certain crowd of Cockneys is bored with *Hamlet*, the Cockneys are not bored because they are too complex and ingenious for *Hamlet*. They feel that the excitement of the saloon bar, of the betting ring, of the newspaper, of the topical music hall, is more complex and ingenious than *Hamlet*; and so it is.

In the absolutely strict sense of the word, the Cockneys are too aesthetic to enjoy *Hamlet*. They have goaded and jaded their artistic feelings too much to enjoy anything simply beautiful. They are aesthetes; and the definition of an aesthete is a man who is experienced enough to admire a good picture, but not inexperienced enough to see it. But if you really took simple people, honourable peasants, kind old servants, dreamy tramps, genial thieves, and brigands to see *Hamlet*, they would simply be sorry for Hamlet. That is to say, they would simply appreciate the fact that it was a great tragedy.

Now I believe in the judgment of all uncultivated people; but it is my misfortune that I am the only quite uncultured person in England who writes articles. My brethren are silent. They will not back me up; they have something better to do. But a few days ago when I saw Miss Julie Marlowe and Mr. Sothern give their very able representation of *Hamlet*, certain things came into my mind about the play which I feel sure that the other uncultured persons share with me. But they will not speak; with a strange modesty they hide their lack of cultivation under a bushel.

There is a threadbare joke which calls the gallery in a theatre "the gods". For my part I accept that joke quite seriously. The people in the gallery are the gods. They are the ultimate authority so far as anything human is the ultimate authority. I do not see anything unreasonable in the actor calling upon them with the same gesture with which he calls upon the mountain of Olympus. When the actor looks down, brooding in despair or calling up black Erebus or the evil spirits, then, in such moments, by all means let him bend his black brows and look down upon the stalls. But if there be in any acted play anything to make him lift up his heart to heaven, then in God's name, when he looks up to heaven, let him see the poor.

There is one little point, for instance, upon which I think the public have mistaken Hamlet, not through themselves but through the critics. There is one point on which the uneducated would probably have gone right; only they have been perverted by the educated. I mean this: that everybody in the modern world has talked of Hamlet as a sceptic. The mere fact of seeing the play acted very finely and swiftly by Miss Marlowe and Mr. Sothern has simply swept the last rags of this heresy out of my head. The really interesting thing about Hamlet was that he was not a sceptic at all. He did not doubt at all, except in the sense that every sane man doubts, including popes and crusaders. The primary point is quite clear. If Hamlet had been a sceptic at all there would have been no tragedy of Hamlet. If he had had any scepticism to exercise, he could have exercised it at once upon the highly improbable ghost of his father. He could have called that eloquent person a hallucination, or some other unmeaning thing, have married Ophelia, and gone on eating bread and butter. This is the first evident point.

The tragedy of Hamlet is not that Hamlet is a sceptic. The tragedy of Hamlet is that he is very much too good a philosopher to be a sceptic. His intellect is so clear that it sees at once the rational possibility of ghosts. But the utter mistake of regarding Hamlet as a sceptic has many other instances. The whole theory arose out of quoting stilted passages out of their context, such as "To be or not to be," or (much worse) the passage in which he says with an almost obvious gesture of fatigue, "Why then, 'tis none to you; for there is nothing either bad or good, but thinking makes it so." Hamlet says this because he is getting sick of the society of two silly men; but if anyone wishes to see how entirely opposite is Hamlet's attitude he can see it in the same conversation. If anyone wishes to listen to the words of a man who in the most final sense is not a sceptic, here are his words:

This goodly frame, the earth, seems to me a sterile promontory; this most excellent canopy the air, look you, this brave o'erhanging firmament, this majestical roof fretted with golden fire, why it appears no other thing to me than a foul and pestilent congregation of vapours. What a piece of work is a man! how noble in reason! how infinite in faculty! in form and moving how express and admirable! in action how like an angel! in apprehension how like a god! the beauty of the world! the paragon of animals! And yet, to me, what is this quintessence of dust?

Oddly enough, I have heard this passage quoted as a pessimistic passage. It is, perhaps, the most optimistic passage in all human literature. It is the absolute expression of the ultimate fact of the faith of Hamlet; his faith that, although he cannot see the world is good, yet certainly it is good; his faith that, though he cannot see man as the image of God, yet certainly he is the image of God. The modern, like the modern conception of Hamlet, believes only in mood. But the real Hamlet, like the Catholic Church, believes in reason. Many fine optimists have praised man when they felt like praising him. Only Hamlet has praised man when he felt like kicking him as a monkey of the mud. Many poets, like Shelley and Whitman, have been optimistic when they felt optimistic. Only Shakespeare has been optimistic when he felt pessimistic. This is the definition of a faith. A faith is that which is able to survive a mood. And Hamlet had this from first to last. Early he protests against a law that he recognizes: "O that the Everlasting had not fixed his canon 'gainst self-slaughter." Before the end he declares that our clumsy management will be turned to something, "rough-hew it how we will".

If Hamlet had been a sceptic he would have had an easy life. He would not have known that his moods were moods. He would have called them Pessimism or Materialism, or some silly name. But Hamlet was a great soul, great enough to know that he was not the world. He knew that there was a truth beyond himself, therefore he believed readily in the things most unlike himself, in Horatio and his ghost. All through his story we can read his conviction that he is wrong. And that to a clear mind like his is only another way of stating that there is something that is right. The real sceptic never thinks he is wrong; for the real sceptic does not think that there is any wrong. He sinks through door after door of a bottomless universe. But Hamlet was the very reverse of a sceptic. He was a thinker.

The Grave-digger

In looking over some medieval books in the beautiful Rylands Library at Manchester I was struck by that perfection and precision in the decorative illumination which so many have praised and so few have realized in this industrious medieval art. But I was even more affected by a quality that belongs at once to the simplest and the soundest human feeling. Plato held this view, and so does every child. Plato held, and the child holds, that the most important thing about a ship (let us say) is that it is a ship. Thus, all these pictures are designed to express things in their quiddity. If these old artists draw a ship, everything is sacrificed to expressing the "shipishness" of the ship. If they draw a tower, its whole object is to be towering. If they draw a flower, its whole object is to be flowering. Their pencils often go wrong as to how the thing looks; their intellects never go wrong as to what the thing is.

These pictures are childish in the proper and complimentary sense of the word. They are childish in this sense, that they are Platonists. When we are very young and vigorous and human we believe in things; it is only when we are very old and dissolute and decaying that we believe in the aspects of things. To see a thing in aspects is to be crippled, to be defective. A full and healthy man realizes a thing called a ship; he realizes it simultaneously from all sides and with all senses. One of his senses tells him that the ship is tall or white, another that the ship is moving or standing still, another that it is battling with broken and noisy waves, another that it is surrounded and soaked with the smell of the sea. But a deaf man would only know that the ship was moving by the passing of objects. A blind man would only know that the ship was moving by the sound of the swirling water. A blind and deaf man would only know that a ship was moving by the fact that he was seasick. This is the thing called "impressionism", that typically modern thing.

Impressionism means shutting up all of one's nine million organs and avenues of appreciation except one. Impressionism means that, whereas Nature has made our senses and impressions support each other, we desire to suppress one part of perception and employ the others. Impressionism, in short, may be justly summarized as "winking the other eye". The Impressionist desires to treat mankind as a brood of the Cyclops. It is not surprising that Whistler wore a monocle; his philosophy was monocular. But the vice is not confined to the pictorial impressionist who deals with visible powers. Just as the painter of that type asks us to use only one of our eyes, so the poet of that type asks us to use only one lobe of our brain.

The characteristic of the finest and most typical modern plays is that they rule out altogether any element inconsistent with their subtle theme. I might almost say with their secret theme. The laughter is excluded at the box-office. A man may say of *Hamlet* or of *Romeo and Juliet* that the tragedy seems to him inadequate. But at least he must allow that this tragedy has been at least adequate to admit and to overshadow comedy. Hamlet's dignity may be destroyed by the German critic; but at least Hamlet's dignity is not destroyed by the Grave-digger. Hamlet meets the Grave-digger, and realizes quite as well as any modern that serious things can be laughed at even by those who are closest to them. The hilarious song of the Grave-digger is the great heroic song of all human democracy, and the first few notes of that cry would have cracked from end to end, like the blast of cock crow, the whole world of Pelleas and Melisande.

There are some who say that Shakespeare was vitally anti-democratic, because every now and then he curses the rabble—as if every lover of the people had not often had cause to curse the rabble. For this is the very definition of

the rabble—it is the people when the people are undemocratic. But if anyone fancies that Shakespeare did not, consciously or unconsciously, realize the rude veracity and
violent humour of the people, the complete answer is to be
found in the mere figure of the Grave-digger. "Has this
fellow no feeling of his business, that he sings at grave-
making?" In that Shakespeare has shown the utter inferior-
ity of Hamlet to the Grave-digger. Hamlet by himself might
almost be a character in Maeterlinck. He wishes to make the
play of *Hamlet* a Maeterlinck play—united, artistic, melancholy, in a monotone. He wishes the Grave-digger to be sad
at his grave-digging; he wishes the Grave-digger to be in the
picture. But the Grave-digger refused to be in the picture,
and the grave-digger will always refuse. The common man,
engaged in tragic occupation, has always refused and will
always refuse, to be tragic.

If anybody really understands the London poor he will
admit that there are two things that really strike him—first,
the persistent tragedy of the poor; and secondly, their persistent farce and their persistent frivolity. Fortunately for the
world, these men have the power of raising a riotous carol of
satire out of the deep pit in which they dig. Fortunately for
the world, they have so little feeling of their business that
they sing at grave-making. Shakespeare showed that he was
not incapable of the ultimate comprehension of democracy
when he made the hind happy and the prince a failure. Many
have criticized the chaos of corpses that occurs at the end of
Hamlet. But, after all, nobody professes to have found the
corpse of the Grave-digger among the debris. If poets have
made their tragedies out of kings it was partly not out of
servility, but out of pity. The man who has dug and drained
and ploughed and cut wood from the beginning of the world
has lived under innumerable Governments, sometimes
good and generally bad. But, as far as we have ever heard of
him, he has always sung at his work. The grave-diggers, the
poor men, always sang at their work when they were building

65

the tombs of the Pharaohs. And in our civilized modern cities they are still singing at their work, although the graves that they are digging are their own.

My rambling meditations began among the Gothic illuminations of the Rylands Library, and they may very rightly end there. In all these pictured and painted medieval Bibles or missals there are traces of many fancies and fashions, but there is not even the trace of a trace of this one modern heresy of artistic monotone. There is not the trace of a trace of this idea of the keeping of comedy out of tragedy. The moderns who disbelieve in Christianity treat it much more reverently than these Christians who did believe in Christianity. The wildest joke in Voltaire is not wilder than some of the jokes coloured here by men, meek and humble, in their creed.

To mention one thing out of a thousand, take this. I have seen a picture in which the seven-headed beast of the Apocalypse was included among the animals in Noah's Ark, and duly provided with a seven-headed wife to assist him in propagating that important race to be in time for the Apocalypse. If Voltaire had thought of that, he would certainly have said it. But the restrictions of these men were restrictions of external discipline; they were not like ours, restrictions of mood. It might be a question how far people should be allowed to make jokes about Christianity; but there was no doubt that they should be allowed to feel jokes about it. There was no question of that merely impressional theory that we should look through only one peep-hole at a time. Their souls were at least stereoscopic. They had nothing to do with that pictorial impressionism which means closing one eye. They had nothing to do with that philosophical impressionism which means being half-witted.

On a Humiliating Heresy

Many modern people like to be regarded as slaves. I mean the most dismal and degraded sort or slaves; moral and spiritual slaves. Popular preachers and fashionable novelists can safely repeat that men are only what their destiny makes them, and that there is no choice or challenge in the lot of man. Dean Inge declares, with a sort of gloomy glee, that some absurd American statistics or experiments show that heredity is an incurable disease and that education is no cure for it. Mr. Arnold Bennett has said that many of his friends drink too much; but that it cannot be helped because they cannot help it. I am not Puritanic about drink; I have drunk all sorts of things; and in my youth, often more than was good for me. But in any conceivable condition, drunk or sober, I should be furious at the suggestion that I could not help it. I should have wanted to punch the head of the consoling fatalist who told me so. Yet nobody seems to punch the heads of consoling fatalists. This, which seems to me the most elementary form of self-respect, seems to be the one thing about which even the sensitive are insensible. These modern persons are very sensitive about some things. They would be furious if somebody said they were not gentlemen; though there is really no more historical reason for pretending that every man is a gentleman than that every man is a marquis, or a man-at-arms. They are frightfully indignant if we say they are not Christians, though they hold themselves free to deny or doubt every conceivable idea of Christianity, even the historical existence of Christ. In the current cant of journalism and politics, they would almost prosecute us for slander if we said they were not Democrats; though any number of them actually prefer aristocracy or autocracy, and

67

the real Democrats in English society are rather a select few. We might almost say that the true believers in democracy are themselves an aristocracy. About all these words men can be morbidly excitable and touchy. They must not be called pagans or plebeians or plain men or reactionaries or oligarchs. But they may be called slaves; they may be called monkeys; and, above all, they may be called machines. One would imagine that the really intolerable insult to human dignity would be to say that human life is not determined by human will. But so long as we do not say they are heathen, we may say they are not human. We may say that they develop as blindly as a plant or turn as automatically as a wheel.

There are all sorts of ways in which this humiliating heresy expresses itself. One is the perpetual itch to describe all crime as lunacy. Now, quite apart from virtue, I would much rather be thought a criminal than a criminal lunatic. As a point not of virtue but of vanity, I should be less insulted by the title of a murderer than by the title of a homicidal maniac. The murderer might be said, not unfairly, to have lost the first fragrance of his innocence, and all that keeps the child near to the cherubim. But the maniac has lost more than innocence; he has lost essence; the complete personality that makes him a man. Yet everybody is talking as if it would be quite natural, and even nice, to be excused for immorality on the ground of idiocy. The principle is applied, with every flourish of liberality and charity, to personalities whom one would imagine quite proud of being personal. It is applied not only to the trivial and transient villains of real life, but to the far more solid and convincing villains of romance.

A distinguished doctor has written a book about the madmen of Shakespeare. By which he did not mean those few fantastic and manifest madmen, whom we might almost call professional madmen, who merely witnessed to the late Elizabethan craze for lurid and horrible grotesques. Ford or

Webster, or some of their fellows, would hardly have hesitated to have a ballet or chorus of maniacs, like a chorus of fairies or fashionable beauties. But the medical gentleman seems to have said that any number of the serious characters were mad. Macbeth was mad; Hamlet was mad; Ophelia was congenitally mad; and so on. If Hamlet was really mad, there does not seem much point in his pretending to be mad. If Ophelia was always mad, there does not seem much point in her going mad. But anyhow, I think a saner criticism will always maintain that Hamlet was sane. He must be sane even in order to be sad; for when we get into a world of complete unreality, even tragedy is unreal. No lunatic ever had so good a sense of humour as Hamlet. A homicidal maniac does not say, "Your wisdom would show itself more richer to signify that to his doctor"; he is a little too sensitive on the subject of doctors. The whole point of Hamlet is that he is really saner than anybody else in the play; though I admit that being sane is not identical with what some call being sensible. Being outside the world, he sees all round it; where everybody else sees his own side of the world, his own worldly ambition, or hatred or love. But, after all, Hamlet pretended to be mad in order to deceive fools. We cannot complain if he has succeeded.

But, whatever we may say about Hamlet, we must not say this about Macbeth. Hamlet was only a mild sort of murderer; a more or less accidental and parenthetical murderer; an amateur. But Macbeth was a good, solid, serious, self-respecting murderer; and we must not have any nonsense about him. For the play of *Macbeth* is, in the supreme and special sense, the Christian Tragedy; to be set against the Pagan Tragedy of Oedipus. It is the whole point about Oedipus that he does not know what he is doing. And it is the whole point about Macbeth that he does know what he is doing. It is not a tragedy of Fate but a tragedy of Freewill. He is tempted of a devil, but he is not driven by a destiny. If the actor pronounces the words properly, the whole audience ought to feel that the story may yet have an entirely new ending, when Macbeth says suddenly, "We will proceed no further in this business." The incredible confusion of modern thought is always suggesting that any indication that men have been influenced is an indication that they have been forced. All men are always being influenced; for every incident is an influence. The question is, which incident shall we allow to be most influential. Macbeth was influenced; but he consented to be influenced. He was not, like a blind tragic pagan, obeying something he thought he ought to obey. He does not worship the Three Witches like the Three Fates. He is a good enlightened Christian, and sins against the light.

The fancy for reading fatalism into this play, where it is most absent, is probably due to the fallacy of a series; or three things in a row. It misleads Macbeth's critics just as it misleads Macbeth. Almost all our pseudo-science proceeds on the principle of saying that one thing follows on another thing, and then dogmatizing about the third thing that is to follow. The whole argument about the Superman, for instance, as developed by Nietzsche and other sophists, depends entirely on this trick of the incomplete triad. First the scientist or sophist asserts that when there was a monkey, there was bound to be a man. Then he simply prophesies that something will follow the man, as the man followed the monkey. This is exactly the trick used by the Witches in Macbeth. They give him first a fact he knows already, that he is Thane of Glamis; then one fact really confirmed in the future, that he is Thane of Cawdor; and then something that is not a fact at all, and need never be a fact at all, unless he chooses to make it one out of his own murderous fancy. This false series, seeming to point at something, though the first term is trivial and the last untrue, does certainly mislead many with a fallacious sense of fate. It has been used by materialists in many ways to destroy the sense of moral liberty; and it has murdered many things besides Duncan.

The Macbeths

In studying any general tragedy the first question necessarily
is what part of tragedy is eternal. If there be any element in
man's work which is in any sense permanent it must have this
characteristic, that it rebukes first one generation and then
another, but rebukes them always in opposite directions and
for opposite faults. The ideal world is always sane. The real
world is always mad. But it is mad about a different thing
every time; all the things that have been are changing and
inconstant. The only thing that is really reliable is the thing
that has never been. All very great classics of art are a rebuke
to extravagance not in one direction but in all directions. The
figure of a Greek Venus is a rebuke to the fat women of
Rubens and also a rebuke to the thin women of Aubrey
Beardsley. In the same way, Christianity, which in its early
years fought the Manicheans because they did not believe in
anything but spirit, has now to fight the Manicheans because
they do not believe in anything but matter. This is perhaps
the test of a very great work of classic creation, that it can be
attacked on inconsistent grounds, and that it attacks its enemies
on inconsistent grounds. Here is a broad and simple test. If
you hear a thing being accused of being too tall and too short,
too red and too green, too bad in one way and too bad also in
the opposite way, then you may be sure that it is very good.

This preface is essential if we are to profit by the main
meaning of *Macbeth*. For the play is so very great that it
covers much more than it appears to cover; it will certainly
survive our age as it has survived its own; it will certainly
leave the twentieth century behind as calmly and completely as it has left the seventeenth century behind. Hence
if we ask for the meaning of this classic we must necessarily

ask the meaning for our own time. It might have another shade of meaning for another period of time. If, as is possible, there should be a barbaric return and if history is any kind of guide, it will destroy everything else before it destroys great literature. The high and civilized sadness of Virgil was enjoyed literally through the darkest instant of the Dark Ages. Long after a wealthier generation has destroyed Parliament they will retain Shakespeare. Men will enjoy the greatest tragedy of Shakespeare even in the thick of the greatest tragedy of Europe.

It is quite possible that Shakespeare may come to be enjoyed by men far simpler than the men for whom he wrote. Voltaire called him a great savage; we may come to the time far darker than the Dark Ages when he will really be enjoyed by savages. Then the story of Macbeth will be read by a man in the actual position of Macbeth. Then the Thane of Glamis may profit by the disastrous superstitions of the Thane of Cawdor. Then the Thane of Cawdor may really resist the impulse to be King of Scotland. There would be a very simple but a real moral if Macbeth could read *Macbeth*. "Do not listen to evil spirits; do not let your ambition run away with you; do not murder old gentlemen in bed; do not kill other people's wives and children as a part of diplomacy; for if you do these things it is highly probable that you will have a bad time." That is the lesson that Macbeth would have learnt from *Macbeth*; that is the lesson that some barbarians of the future may possibly learn from *Macbeth*. And it is a true lesson. Great work has something to say quite simply to the simple. The barbarians would understand *Macbeth* as a solid warning against vague and violent ambition; and it is such a warning, and they would take along with it this lesson also, which is none the worse because perhaps only the barbarians could adequately understand it. "Distrust those malevolent spirits who speak flatteringly to you. They are not benevolent spirits; if they were they would be more likely to beat you about the head."

Before we talk then of the lesson of a great work of art, let us realize that it has a different lesson for different ages, because it is itself eternal. And let us realize that such a lesson will be in our own day not absolute but suited to the particular vices or particular misfortunes of that day. We are not in any danger at the moment of the positive and concrete actions which correspond to those of *Macbeth*. The good old habit of murdering kings (which was the salvation of so many commonwealths in the past) has fallen into desuetude. The idea of such a play must be for us (and for our sins) more subtle. The idea is more subtle but it is almost inexpressibly great. Let us before reading the play consider if only for a moment what is the main idea of *Macbeth* for modern men.

One great idea on which all tragedy builds is the idea of the continuity of human life. The one thing a man cannot do is exactly what all modern artists and free lovers are always trying to do. He cannot cut his life up into separate sections. The case of the modern claim for freedom in love is the first and most obvious that occurs to the mind; therefore I use it for this purpose of illustration. You cannot have an idyll with Maria and an episode with Jane; there is no such thing as an episode. There is no such thing as an idyll. It is idle to talk about abolishing the tragedy of marriage when you cannot abolish the tragedy of sex. Every flirtation is a marriage; it is a marriage in this frightful sense; that it is irrevocable. I have taken this case of sexual relations as one out of a hundred; but of any case in human life the thing is true. The basis of all tragedy is that man lives a coherent and continuous life. It is only a worm that you can cut in two and leave the severed parts still alive. You can cut a worm up into episodes and they are still living episodes. You can cut a worm up into idylls and they are quite brisk and lively idylls. You can do all this to him precisely because he is a worm. You cannot cut a man up and leave him kicking, precisely because he is a man. We know this because man even in his lowest and

73

darkest manifestation has always this characteristic of physical and psychological unity. His identity continues long enough to see the end of many of his own acts; he cannot be cut off from his past with a hatchet; as he sows so shall he reap.

This then is the basis of all tragedy, this living and perilous continuity which does not exist in the lower creatures. This is the basis of tragedy, and this is certainly the basis of *Macbeth*. The great ideas of *Macbeth*, uttered in the first few scenes with a tragic energy which has never been equalled perhaps in Shakespeare or out of him, is the idea of the enormous mistake a man makes if he supposes that one decisive act will clear his way. Macbeth's ambition, though selfish and someway sullen, is not in itself criminal or morbid. He wins the title of Glamis in honourable war; he deserves and gets the title of Cawdor; he is rising in the world and has a not ignoble exhilaration in doing so. Suddenly a new ambition is presented to him (of the agency and atmosphere which presents it I shall speak in a moment) and he realizes that nothing lies across his path to the Crown of Scotland except the sleeping body of Duncan. If he does that one cruel thing, he can be infinitely kind and happy.

Here, I say, is the first and most formidable of the great actualities of *Macbeth*. You cannot do a mad thing in order to reach sanity. Macbeth's mad resolve is not a cure even for his own irresolution. He was indecisive before his decision. He is, if possible, more indecisive after he has decided. The crime does not get rid of the problem. Its effect is so bewildering that one may say that the crime does not get rid of the temptation. Make a morbid decision and you will only become more morbid; do a lawless thing and you will only get into an atmosphere much more suffocating than that of law. Indeed, it is a mistake to speak of a man as "breaking out". The lawless man never breaks out; he breaks in. He smashes a door and finds himself in another room, he smashes a wall and finds himself in a yet smaller one. The more he shatters the more his habitation shrinks. Where he ends you may read in the end of *Macbeth*.

For us, moderns, therefore, the first philosophical significance of the play is this; that our life is one thing and that our lawless acts limit us; every time we break a law we make a limitation. In some strange way hidden in the deeps of human psychology, if we build our palace on some unknown wrong it turns very slowly into our prison. Macbeth at the end of the play is not merely a wild beast; he is a caged wild beast. But if this is the thing to be put in a primary position there is something else that demands at least our second one. The second idea in the main story of *Macbeth* is, of course, that of the influence of evil suggestion upon the soul, particularly evil suggestion of a mystical and transcendental kind. In this connection the mystical character of the promptings is not more interesting than the mystical character of the man to whom they are especially sent. Mystical promptings are naturally sweet to a mystic. The character of Macbeth in this regard has been made the matter of a great deal of brilliant and futile discussion. Some critics have represented him as a burly silent soldier because he won battles for his country. Other critics have represented him as a feverish and futile decadent because he makes long practical speeches full of the most elaborate imagery. In the name of commonsense let it be remembered that Shakespeare lived before the time when unsuccessful poets thought it poetical to be decadent and unsuccessful soldiers thought it military to be silent. Men like Sidney and Raleigh and Essex could have fought as well as Macbeth and could have ranted as well as Macbeth. Why should Shakespeare shrink from making a great general talk poetry when half the great generals of his time actually wrote great poetry?

The whole legend, therefore, which some critics have based on the rich rhetoric of *Macbeth*: the legend that Macbeth was a febrile and egotistical coward because he liked the sound of his own voice, may be dismissed as a manifestation of the diseases of later days. Shakespeare meant Macbeth for a fine orator for he made fine speeches; he also meant him for a fine soldier because he made him not only win battles bravely, but what is much more to the point, lose battles bravely; he made him, when overwhelmed by enemies in heaven and earth, die the death of a hero. But Macbeth is meant to be among other things an orator and a poet; and it is to Macbeth in this capacity that the evil supernatural appeal is made. If there be any such thing as evil influences coming from beyond the world, they have never been so suggestively indicated as they are here. They appeal, as evil always does, to the existence of a coherent and comprehensible scheme. It is the essence of a nightmare that it turns the whole cosmos against us. Two of their prophecies have been fulfilled; may it not be assumed then that the third will also be fulfilled?

Also they appeal, as evil always does (being slavish itself and believing all men slaves) to the inevitable. They put Macbeth's good fortune before him as if it were not so much a fortune as a fate. In the same way imperialists sought to salve the consciences of Englishmen by giving them the offer of gold and empire with all the gloom of predestination. When the devil, and the witches who are the servants of the devil, wish to make a weak man snatch a crown that does not belong to him, they are too cunning to come to him and say, "Will you be King?" They say without further parley, "All hail, Macbeth, that shall be king hereafter." This weakness Macbeth really has; that he is easily attracted by that kind of spiritual fatalism which relieves the human creature of a great part of his responsibility. In this way there is a strange and sinister appropriateness in the way in which the promises of the evil spirits end in new fantasies; end, so to speak, as mere diabolical jokes. Macbeth accepts as a piece of unreasoning fate first his crime and then his crown. It is appropriate that this fate which he has accepted as external and irrational should end in incidents of mere extravagant bathos, in the walking forest and strange birth of Macduff. He has once surrendered himself with a kind of dark and evil faith, to a machinery of destiny that he can neither respect nor understand, and it is the proper sequel of this that the machinery should produce a situation which crushes him as something useless.

Shakespeare does not mean that Macbeth's emotionalism and rich rhetoric prove him to be unmanly in any ordinary sense. But Shakespeare does mean, I think, to suggest that the man, virile in his essential structure, has this weak spot in his artistic temperament; that fear of the mere strength of destiny and of unknown spirits, of their strength as apart from their virtue, which is the only proper significance of the word superstition. No man can be superstitious who loves his God, even if the god be Mumbo-Jumbo. Macbeth has something of this fear and fatalism; and fatalism is exactly the point at which rationalism passes silently into superstition. Macbeth, in short, has any amount of physical courage, he has even a great deal of moral courage. But he lacks what may be called spiritual courage; he lacks a certain freedom and dignity of the human soul in the universe, a freedom and dignity which one of the scriptural writers expresses as the difference between the servants and the sons of God.

But the man Macbeth and his marked but inadequate manliness, can only be expressed in connection with the character of his wife. And the question of Lady Macbeth immediately arouses again the controversies that have surrounded this play. Miss Ellen Terry and Sir Henry Irving acted *Macbeth* upon the theory that Macbeth was a feeble and treacherous man and that Lady Macbeth was a frail and clinging woman. A somewhat similar view of Lady Macbeth has been, I believe, consistently uttered by a distinguished American actress. The question as commonly stated, in short, is the question of whether Macbeth was really masculine, and second, of whether Lady Macbeth was not really feminine. The old critics assumed that because Lady

Macbeth obviously ruled her husband she must have been a masculine woman. The whole inference of course is false. Masculine women may rule the Borough Council, but they never rule their husbands. The women who rule their husbands are the feminine women and I am entirely in accord with those who think that Lady Macbeth must have been a very feminine woman. But while some critics rightly insist on the feminine character of Lady Macbeth they endeavour to deprive Macbeth of that masculine character which is obviously the corollary of the other. They think Lady Macbeth must be a man because she rules. And on the same idiotic principle they think that Macbeth must be a woman or a coward or a decadent or something odd because he is ruled. The most masculine kind of man always is ruled. As a friend of mine once said, very truly, physical cowards are the only men who are not afraid of women.

The real truth about Macbeth and his wife is somewhat strange but cannot be too strongly stated. Nowhere else in all his wonderful works did Shakespeare describe the real character of the relations of the sexes so sanely, or so satisfactorily as he describes it here. The man and the woman are never more normal than they are in the abnormal and horrible story. *Romeo and Juliet* does not better describe love than this describes marriage. The dispute that goes on between Macbeth and his wife about the murder of Duncan is almost word for word a dispute which goes on at any suburban breakfast-table about something else. It is merely a matter of changing "Infirm of purpose, give me the daggers" into "Infirm of purpose, give me the postage stamps." And it is quite a mistake to suppose that the woman is to be called masculine or even in any exclusive sense strong. The strengths of the two partners differ in kind. The woman has more of that strength on the spot which is called industry. The man has more of that strength in reserve which is called laziness.

But the acute truth of this actual relation is much deeper even than that. Lady Macbeth exhibits one queer and astounding kind of magnanimity which is quite peculiar to women. That is, she will take something that her husband dares not do but which she knows he wants to do and she will become more fierce for it than he is. For her, as for all very feminine souls (that is, very strong ones) selfishness is the only thing which is acutely felt as sin: she will commit any crime if she is not committing it only for herself. Her husband thirsts for the crime egotistically and therefore vaguely, darkly, and subconsciously, as a man becomes conscious of the beginnings of physical thirst. But she thirsts for the crime altruistically and therefore clearly and sharply, as a man perceives a public duty to society. She puts the thing in plain words, with an acceptance of extremes. She has that perfect and splendid cynicism of women which is the most terrible thing God has made. I say it without irony and without any undue enjoyment of its slight element of humour.

If you want to know what are the permanent relations of the married man with the married woman you cannot read it anywhere more accurately than in the little domestic idyll of Mr. and Mrs. Macbeth. Of a man so male and a woman so female, I cannot believe anything except that they ultimately save their souls. Macbeth was strong in every masculine sense up to the very last moment; he killed himself in battle. Lady Macbeth was strong in the very female sense which is perhaps a more courageous sense; she killed herself, but not in battle. As I say, I cannot think that souls so strong and so elemental have not retained those permanent possibilities of humility and gratitude which ultimately place the soul in heaven. But wherever they are they are together. For alone among so many of the figures of human fiction, they are actually married.

Realism in Art

What fun it would be if good actors suddenly acted like real people! I do not mean anything about tone, manner, or gesture. The actor does not behave, even in public life, a scrap more artificially than does many a minister, parson or politician, even in private life. Every man has an accent; and no man knows he has it. Every man has an accent: and, to that extent, every man has an affectation. You and I are at least always clever enough to speak the speech of our class. Our limitation is that though we can speak it, we cannot hear it. There is no convention of the theatre that may not tomorrow be the convention of the world. There is no conceivable drawl or bleat or bellow from one end of a Surrey melodrama to the other which might not easily become the admitted accent of the best society. Dropping the "h" might be as good English as it is French. Already the ladies on the stage are often less painted than the ladies in the stalls. Already the footlights are a faint and flickering barrier; *il n'y a plus de Pyrénées*. No, I mean nothing about natural or "quietly realistic" acting; that ideal is much too faint and far. When people have begun to act like life in a drawing-room, it will be time enough to ask them to act like life on a stage.

No, I mean something much funnier than that—as the man in Jerome's excellent tale said when he had told the dullest story ever endured by men. I mean the funniest of all earthly things; I mean what I say. I mean what fun it would be if actors suddenly acted as if they were in real life. Suppose they were to act *freely*; to change their minds. Suppose that when Joseph Surface told Lady Teazle to hide behind the screen, she said she wouldn't. Suppose she said there was no harm in visiting so virtuous a gentleman; and that she specially wanted to talk to Sir Peter on a point about the weekly washing. What *would* happen to the great Screen Scene? What would everybody do? Suppose Hamlet ended the soliloquy "To be or not to be" by suddenly deciding not to be. Suppose he really did his quietus make with a bare bodkin. What would the Grave-digger do? What would Osric do? It is awful to think of. Or, to take a far more terrible passage, suppose when Macbeth says, "We will proceed no further in this business"—suppose he stuck to his words! Suppose he declined to be henpecked. Suppose he raised on the stage the red banner of the revolted male against the eternal female tyranny. A gladiatorial show, with real men butchered, would be far less exciting.

We are always hearing about the limits of realism in art; that is, of this or that respect in which a written thing can never be quite like an acted thing. It seems odd to me that nobody ever mentions the chief chasm of cleavage between the thing written and the thing done. It turns on the old pivot of what theologians call Free Will. The difference is that all events in genuine art are decided; all events in genuine life (in anything worth calling life) are undecided. What is written is written (to quote a Roman governor who showed his taste for epigram at a somewhat unlucky moment); what is written is written; but what is doing need not be done. Every artistic drama is named on the first page a tragedy or a comedy. That is because in every artistic drama the last page is written before the first. But it is not so in that terrific drama which Heaven has given us to play upon the earth, without any punctual cues, with a very invisible, and sometimes inaudible prompter, and without the faintest notion about when the curtain will come down. If the drama of real life is more dreadful, it has at least one agreeable quality; it is more uncertain. Every human life begins in tragedy, for it begins in travail. But every human life may end in comedy—even in divine comedy. It may end in a joy beyond all our joys; in that cry across the chasm. "Fear not,

I have conquered the world." Real human life differs from all imitations of it in the fact that it can perpetually alter itself as it goes along. Art can hardly survive one such change. It could not possibly survive a series of such changes. The full cataract of Dickens's creative power was hardly strong enough to carry him round those two or three corners where the stream of his story really altered its course. Of a fictitious story we may say decisively that it should go as straight as possible to its end. Or, to put it another way, the sooner we have finished a novel the better. But of a real story, as distinct from a fictitious story, we may say that the more the stream straggles this way and that, the more likely it is to be a clean or even sacred stream. It proves its wish to go right by so often confessing that it has gone wrong.

I began to think of all these things in the last days of the late performances of Sir Herbert Tree's *Macbeth*. My meditation comes too late. I am one of those who are doomed (an immoral expression) to be always late. I had a relative who came late for the Battle of Waterloo; and I sometimes almost hope that I myself may come late for the Day of Judgment. But though it was at Sir Herbert Tree's performance that I began thinking, I have only just finished thinking. And though I have not always agreed by any means with Sir Herbert's interpretation of great Shakespearian characters, I am bound to say that in this case he gave me, in the middle of a settled and hackneyed story, the electric shock of moral liberty. When he said, "We will proceed no further in this business," for an instant I thought he wouldn't—though I have read *Macbeth* a hundred times. In the midst of life we are in death; in that one dead pageantry, in the midst of death I was in life. I thought for a flash that the play might end differently. Alas! The play was written more than three hundred years ago.

Calvinists objected to stage plays. Yet all stage plays are forced to be Calvinistic. They are forced, by the very nature of art, to damn or save a man from the beginning. That is why the old Greek plays about fatality succeeded. Such dramas were popular in spite of everything that could be unpopular, and everything that could be undramatic—in spite of masks and monologues and a shallow stage and an absence of incident. They suited the drama because they were full of destiny. And yet I still think that the greatest drama of all is that in which the throne of destiny is shaken for an instant. I think the greatest drama in the world is *Macbeth*.

I think *Macbeth* the one supreme drama because it is the one Christian drama; and I will accept the accusation of prejudice. But I mean by Christian (in this matter) the strong sense of spiritual liberty and of sin; the idea that the best man can be as bad as he chooses. You may call Othello a victim of chance. You may call Hamlet a victim of temperament. You cannot call Macbeth anything but a victim of Macbeth. The evil spirits tempt him but they never force him; they never even frighten him, for he is a very brave man. I have often wondered that no one has made so obvious a parallel as that between the murders of Macbeth and the marriages of Henry VIII. Both Henry and Macbeth were originally brave good-humoured men, better rather than worse than their neighbours. Both Henry and Macbeth hesitated over their first crime—the first stabbing and the first divorce. Both found out the fate which is in evil—for Macbeth went on murdering and poor Henry went on marrying. There is only one fault in the parallel. Unfortunately for history, Henry VIII was not deposed.

The Tragedy of King Lear

The tragedy of *King Lear*, in some of its elements perhaps the very greatest of all the Shakespearian tragedies, is relatively seldom played. It is even possible to have a dark suspicion that it is not universally read; with the usual deplorable result: that it is universally quoted. Perhaps nothing has done so much to weaken the greatest of English achievements, and to leave it open to facile revolt or fatigued reaction, than the abominable habit of quoting Shakespeare without reading Shakespeare. It has encouraged all that pompous theatricality which first created an idolatry and then an iconoclasm; all that florid tradition in which old playgoers and after-dinner speakers talked about the Bard or the Swan of Avon, until it was comparatively easy, at the end of the Victorian era, for somebody like Bernard Shaw to propose an Edwardian massacre of Bards and almost to insinuate that the swan was a goose. Most of the trouble came from what are called Familiar Quotations, which were hardly even representative or self-explanatory quotations. In almost all the well-known passages from Shakespeare, to quote the passage is to miss the point. It is almost needless to note what may be called the vulgar examples; as in the case of those who say that Shakespeare asks, "What is in a name?"; which is rather like saying that Shakespeare says murder must be done, and it were best if it were done quickly. The popular inference always is that Shakespeare thought that names do not matter; there being possibly no man on God's earth who was less likely to think so, than the man who made such magnificent mouthfuls out of mandragora and hurricanes, of the names of Hesperides or Hercules. The remark has no point, except in the purely personal circumstances in which it has poignancy, in the mouth of a girl commanded to hate a man she loves, because of a name that seems to her to have nothing to do with him. The play now under consideration is no exception to this disastrous rule. The old woman who complained that the tragedy of *Hamlet* was so full of quotations would have found almost as many in the tragedy of *King Lear*. And they would have had the same character as those from *Hamlet* or *Romeo and Juliet*; that those who leave out the context really leave out the conception. They have a mysterious power of making the world weary of a few fixed and disconnected words, and yet leaving the world entirely ignorant of the real meaning of those words.

Thus, in the play of *King Lear*, there are certain words which everybody has heard hundreds of times, in connections either intentionally or unintentionally absurd. We have all read or heard of somebody saying, "How sharper than a serpent's tooth it is to have a thankless child." Somehow the very words sound as if they were mouthed by some tipsy actor or silly and senile person in a comic novel. I do not know why these particular words, as words, should be selected for citation. Shakespeare was a casual writer; he was often especially careless about metaphors, careless about making them and careless about mixing them. There is nothing particularly notable about this particular metaphor of the tooth; it might just as well have been a wolf's tooth or a tiger's tooth. The lines quoted only become remarkable when we read them with the rest of the scene, and with a very much more remarkable passage, which is never quoted at all. The whole point of Lear's remark is that, when buffeted by the first insult of Goneril, he breaks forth into a blasting bodily curse upon the woman, praying first that she may have no children, then that she may have horrible and unnatural children, that she may give birth to a monstrosity, *that she may feel how*, etc. Without that terrible implication, the serpent is entirely harmless and his teeth are drawn. I cannot imagine why only the weakest lines in the speech are everlastingly repeated, and the strongest lines in it are never mentioned at all.

A man might well harden into the horrid suspicion that most people have hardly read the play at all, when he remembers how many things there are in it that are not repeated, and yet would certainly be remembered. There are things in it that no man who has read them can ever forget. Amid all the thunders of the storm, it comes like a new clap of thunder, when the thought first crosses the mad king's mind that he must not complain of wind and storm and lightning, because they are not his daughters. "I never gave you kingdoms, called you children." And I imagine that the great imaginative invention of the English, the thing called Nonsense, never rose to such a height and sublimity of unreason and horror, as when the Fool juggles with time and space and tomorrow and yesterday, as he says soberly at the end of his rant: "This prophecy Merlin shall make; for I live before his time." This is one of the Shakespearian shocks or blows that take the breath away. But in the same scene of the storm and the desolate wandering, there is another example of the sort of thing I mean in the matter of quotation. It is not so strong an example, because the words are very beautiful in themselves; and have often been applied beautifully to pathetic human circumstances not unworthy of them. Nevertheless, they are something not only superior, but quite startlingly different, in the circumstances in which they really stand. We have all of us heard a hundred times that some unlucky law-breaker, or more or less pardonable profligate, was "more sinned against than sinning". But the words thus used have not a hundredth part of the point and power of the words as used by Lear. The point of the passage is that he himself challenges the cosmic powers to a complete examination; that he finds in his despair a sort of dizzy detachment of the intellect, and strikes the balance to his own case with a kind of insane impartiality. Regarding the storm that rages round him as a universal rending and uprooting of everything, something that will pluck out the roots of all things, even the darkest and foulest roots of the heart of man deceitful above all things and desperately wicked, he affirms in the face of the most appalling self-knowledge, clear and blasting as the lightning, that his sufferings must still be greater than his sins. It is possibly the most tremendous thing a man ever said; whether or no any man had the right to say it. It would be hard to beat it even in the Book of Job. And it does weaken the particular strength of it that it should be used, however sympathetically, as a cheerful and charitable guess about the weaknesses of other people.

There are certain abstractions very strong in Shakespeare's mind, without which his plays are much misunderstood by modern people, who look to them for nothing whatever except realistic detail about individuals. For instance, there runs through the whole play of *King Lear*, as there runs through the whole play of *Richard the Second*, an abstraction which was an actuality of awful vividness to the man of Shakespeare's time; the idea of The King. Under the name of Divine Right, a very unlucky name, it was mixed up with Parliamentary and sectarian quarrels which afterwards altogether dwarfed and diminished its dignity. But Divine Right was originally much more human than that. It resolved itself roughly into this; that there are three forms in which men can accept the idea of justice or the authority of the commonwealth: in the form of an assembly, in the form of a document, or in the form of a man. King Lear is a man; but he is or has been a sacramental or sacred man; and that is why he can be a desecrated man. Even those who prefer to be governed by the scroll of the law, or by the assembly of the tribe, must understand that men have wished, and may again wish, to be governed by a man; and that where this wish has existed the man does become, not indeed divine, but certainly different. It is not an accident that Lear is a king as well as a father, and that Goneril and Regan are not only daughters but traitors. Treason, or what is felt as treason, does break the heart of the world; and it has seldom been so nearly broken as here.

Part Three: The Comedies

Shakespeare and the Legal Lady

I wonder how long liberated woman will endure the invidious ban which excludes her from being a hangman. Or rather, to speak with more exactitude, a hangwoman. The very fact that there seems something vaguely unfamiliar and awkward about the word, is but a proof of the ages of sex oppression that have accustomed us to this sex privilege. The ambition would not perhaps have been understood by the prudish and sentimental heroines of Fanny Burney and Jane Austen. But it is now agreed that the further we go beyond these faded proprieties the better; and I really do not see how we could go further. There are always torturers of course, who will probably return under some scientific name. Obscurantists may use the old argument that woman has never risen to the first rank in this or other arts; that Jack Ketch was not Jemima Ketch, and that the headsman was called Samson and not Delilah. And they will be overwhelmed with the old report that until we have hundreds of healthy women happily engaged in this healthful occupation, it will be impossible to judge whether they can rise above the average or no. Tearful sentimentalists may feel something unpleasing, something faintly repugnant about the new feminine trade. But, as the indignant policewoman said the other day, when a magistrate excluded some of her sex and service from revolting revelations, "crime is a disease", and must be studied scientifically however hideous it may be. Death also is a disease and frequently a fatal one. Experiments must be made in it and it must be inflicted in any form, however hideous, in a cool and scientific manner.

It is not true, of course, that crime is a disease. It is criminology that is a disease. But the suggestion about the painful duties of a policewoman leads naturally to my deduction about the painful duties of a hangwoman. And I make it in the faint hope of waking up some of the feminists, that they may at least be moved to wonder what they are doing and to attempt to find out. What they are not doing is obvious enough. They are not asking themselves two perfectly plain questions; first, whether they want anybody to be a hangman; and second, whether they want everybody to be a hangman. They simply assume, with panting impetuosity, that we want everybody to be everything, criminologists, constables, barristers, executioners, torturers. It never seems to them that some of us doubt the beauty and blessedness of these things, and are rather glad to limit them like other necessary evils. And this applies especially to the doubtful though defensible case of the advocate.

There is one phrase perpetually repeated and now practically stereotyped, which to my mind concentrates and sums up all the very worst qualities in the very worst journalism; all its paralysis of thought, all its monotony of chatter, all its sham culture and shoddy picturesqueness, all its perpetual readiness to cover any vulgarity of the present with any sentimentalism about the past. There is one phrase that does measure to how low an ebb the mind of my unfortunate profession can sink. It is the habit of perpetually calling any of the new lady barristers "Portia".

First of all, of course, it is quite clear that the journalist does not know who Portia was. If he has ever heard of the story of the *Merchant of Venice* he has managed to miss the only point of the story. Suppose a man had been so instructed in the story of *As You Like It* that he remained under the impression that Rosalind really was a boy, and was the brother of Celia. We should say that the plot of the comedy had reached his mind in a rather confused form. Suppose a man had seen a whole performance of the play of *Twelfth Night* without discovering the fact that the page called Cesario was really a girl called Viola. We should say that he had succeeded in seeing the play without exactly seeing the point. But there is exactly the same blind stupidity in calling a barrister Portia; or even in calling Portia a barrister. It misses in exactly the same sense the whole meaning of the scene. Portia is no more a barrister than Rosalind is a boy. She is no more the learned jurist whom Shylock congratulates than Viola is the adventurous page whom Olivia loves. The whole point of her position is that she is a heroic and magnanimous fraud. She has not taken up the legal profession, or any profession; she has not sought that public duty, or any public duty. Her action, from first to last, is wholly and entirely private. Her motives are not professional but private. Her ideal is not public but private. She acts as much on personal grounds in the Trial Scene as she does in the Casket Scene. She acts in order to save a friend and especially a friend of the husband whom she loves. Anything less like the attitude of an advocate, for good or evil, could not be conceived. She seeks individually to save an individual and in order to do so is ready to *break* all the existing laws of the profession and the public tribunal; to assume lawlessly powers she has not got, to intrude where she would never be legally admitted, to pretend to be somebody else, to dress up as a man; to do what is actually a crime against the law. This is not what is now called the attitude of a public woman; it is certainly not the attitude of a lady lawyer, any more than of any other kind of lawyer. But it is emphatically the attitude of a private woman; that much more ancient and much more powerful thing.

Suppose that Portia had really become an advocate, merely by advocating the cause of Antonio against Shylock. The first thing that follows is that, as like as not, she would be briefed in the next case to advocate the cause of Shylock against Antonio. She would, in the ordinary way of business, have to help Shylock to punish with ruin the private extravagances of Gratiano. She would have to assist Shylock to distrain on poor Launcelot Gobbo and sell up all his miserable sticks. She might well be employed by him to ruin the happiness of Lorenzo and Jessica, by urging some obsolete parental power or some technical flaw in the marriage service. Shylock evidently had a great admiration for her forensic talents; and indeed that sort of lucid and detached admission of the talents of a successful opponent is a very Jewish characteristic. There seems no reason why he should not have employed her regularly, whenever he wanted some one to recover ruthless interest, to ruin needy households, to drive towards theft or suicide the souls of desperate men. But there seems every reason to doubt whether the Portia whom Shakespeare describes for us is likely to have taken on the job.

Anyhow, that is the job and I am not here arguing that it is not a necessary job. Many honourable men have made an arguable case for the advocate who has to support Shylock, and men much worse than Shylock. But that is the job; and to cover up its ugly realities with a loose literary quotation that really refers to the exact opposite, is one of those crawling and cowardly evasions and verbal fictions which make all this sort of servile journalism so useless for every worthy or working purpose. If we wish to consider whether a lady should be a barrister, we should consider sanely and clearly what a barrister is and what a lady is; and then come to our conclusion according to what we consider worthy or worthless in the traditions of the two things. But the spirit of advertisement, which tries to associate soap with sunlight or grapenuts with grapes, calls to its rescue an old romance of Venice and tries to cover up a practical problem in the robes of a romantic heroine of the stage. This is the sort of confusion that really leads to corruption. In one sense it would matter very little that the legal profession was formally open to women, for it is only a very exceptional sort of woman who would see herself as a vision of beauty in the character of Mr. Sergeant Buzfuz. And most girls are more likely to be stage-struck, and want to be the real Portia on the stage, rather than lawstruck and want to be the very reverse of Portia in a law court. For that matter, it would make relatively little difference if formal permission were given to a woman to be a hangman or a torturer. Very few women would have a taste for it and very few men would have a taste for the women who had a taste for it. But advertisement, by its use of the vulgar picturesque, can hide the realities of this professional problem, as it can hide the realities of tinned meats and patent medicines. It can conceal the fact that the hangman exists to hang, and that the torturer exists to torture. Similarly it can conceal the fact that the Buzfuz barrister exists to bully. It can hide from the innocent female aspirants outside even the perils and potential abuses that would be admitted by the honest male advocate inside. And that is part of a very much larger problem, which extends beyond this particular profession to a great many other professions; and not least to the lowest and most lucrative of all modern professions; that of professional politics.

What is true of the political is equally true of the professional ambition. Much of the mere imitation of masculine tricks and trades is indeed trivial enough; it is a mere masquerade. The greatest of Roman satirists noted that in his day the more fast of the fashionable ladies liked to fight as gladiators in the amphitheatre. In that one statement he pinned and killed, like moths on a cork, a host of women prophets and women pioneers and large-minded liberators of their sex in modern England and America. But besides these more showy she-gladiators there are also multitudes of worthy and sincere women who take the new (or rather old) professions seriously. The only disadvantage is that in many of these professions they can only continue to be serious by ceasing to be sincere. But the simplicity with which they first set out is an enormous support to old and complex and corrupt institutions. No modest person setting out to learn an elaborate science can be expected to start with the

95

assumption that it is not worth learning. The young lady will naturally begin to learn Law as gravely as she begins to learn Greek. It is not in that mood that she will conceive independent doubts about the ultimate relations of Law and Justice. Just as the Suffragettes are already complaining that the realism of industrial revolution interferes with their new hobby of voting, so the lady lawyers are quite likely to complain that the realism of legal reformers interferes with their new hobby of legalism. We are suffering in every department from the same cross-purposes that can be seen in the case of any vulgar patent medicine. In Law and Medicine we have the thing advertised in the public press instead of analysed by the public authority. What we want is not the journalistic Portia but the theatrical Portia, who is also the real Portia. We do not want the woman who will enter the law court with the solemn sense of a lasting vocation. We want a Portia; a woman who will enter it as lightly and leave it as gladly as she did.

The Heroines of Shakespeare

It is an odd thing that the words hero and heroine have in their constant use in connection with literary fiction entirely lost their meaning. A hero now means merely a young man sufficiently decent and reliable to go through a few adventures without hanging himself or taking to drink. The modern realistic novelist introduces us to a weak-kneed young suburban gentleman who varies dull respectability with duller vice, and consumes three thick volumes before he has decided which woman he will marry. And by the strange, blasphemous perversion of words, he is called "The Hero". He might just as well, in reason, be called "The Saint", or "The Prophet", or "The Messiah". A hero means a man of heroic stature, a demigod, a man on whom rests something of the mystery which is beyond man. Now, the great and striking thing about heroines like Portia and Isabella and Rosalind is that they are heroines, that they do represent a certain dignity, a certain breadth, which is distinct from the mere homely vigour of the Shakespearian men. You could not slap Portia on the back as you could Bassanio. There may or may not be a divinity that doth hedge a king, but there is certainly a divinity that doth hedge a queen. To understand this heroic quality in the Shakespearian women it is necessary to grasp a little the whole Elizabethan, and especially the whole Shakespearian, view of this matter.

The great conception at the back of the oldest religions in the world is, of course, the conception that man is of divine origin, a sacred and splendid heir, the eldest son of the universe. But humanity could not in practice carry out this conception that everyone was divine. The practical imagination recoils from the idea of two gods swindling each other over a pound of cheese. The mind refuses to accept the idea of sixty bodies, each filled with a blazing divinity, elbowing each other to get into an omnibus. This mere external difficulty causes men in every age to fall back upon the conception that certain men preserved for other men the sanctity of man. Certain figures were more divine because they were more human. In primitive times of folklore, and in some feudal periods, this larger man was the conquering hero, the strong man who slew dragons and oppressors. To the old Hebrews this sacred being was the prophet; to the men of the Christian ages it was the saint. To the Elizabethans this sacred being was the pure woman.

The heroic conception of womanhood comes out most clearly in Shakespeare because of his astonishing psychological imagination, but it exists as an ideal in all Elizabethans. And the precise reason why the heroines of Shakespeare are so splendid is because they stand alone among all his characters as the embodiments of the primal ages of faith. They are the high and snowy peaks which catch the last rays of the belief in the actual divinity of man. We feel, as we read the plays, that the women are more large, more typical, belong more to an ideal and less to a realistic literature. They are the very reverse of abstractions; considered merely as women they are finished down to the finest detail. Yet there is something more in them that is not in the men. Portia is a good woman and Bassanio is a good man. But Portia is more than a woman: Portia is Woman and Bassanio is not Man. He is merely a very pleasant and respectable individual.

There are Elizabethan plays so dark and frightful that they read like the rubbish from the wastepaper basket of a madhouse. No one but a prophet possessed of devils, one might fancy, could produce incidents so abrupt and so sombre, could call up scenes so graphic and so unmeaning. In one play a man is forced to watch the murder of those he loves and cannot speak because his tongue is nailed to the floor with a dagger. In another a man is torn with red-hot pincers; in another a man is dropped through a broken floor into a cauldron. With horrible cries out of the lowest hell it is proclaimed that man cannot be continent, that man cannot be true, that he is only the filthiest and the funniest of monkeys. And yet the one belief that all these dark and brutal men admit, is the belief in the pure woman. In this one virtue, in this one sex, something heroic and holy, something in the highest sense of that word, fabulous, was felt to reside. Man was natural, but woman was supernatural.

Now it is quite clear that this was the Elizabethan view of woman. Portia is not only the most splendid and magnanimous woman in literature. She is not only the heroine of the play, she is the play. She is the absolute heroic ideal upon which the play is built. Shakespeare had conceived, with extraordinary force, humour and sympathy, a man to express the ideal of technical justice, formal morality, and the claim of a man to his rights: the man was Shylock. Over against him he set a figure representing the larger conception of generosity and persuasion, the justice that is fused of a score of genial passions, the compromise that is born of a hundred worthy enthusiasms. Portia had to represent the ideal of magnanimity in law, morality, religion, art and politics. And Shakespeare made this figure a good woman because, to the mind of his day, to make it a good woman was to ring it with a halo and arm it with a sword.

The Repetition of Rosalind

In numberless modern novels and magazine stories, the heroine is apparently complimented by being described as "boyish". Doubtless there will soon be another fashion in fiction, in which the hero will always be described as girlish. Fettered as we are with an antiquated Victorian prejudice of the equality of the sexes, we cannot quite understand why one should be a compliment any more than the other. But, anyhow, the present fashion offers a much deeper difficulty. For the girl is being complimented on her boyishness by people who obviously know nothing at all about boys. Nothing could possibly be more unlike a boy than the candid, confident, unconventional and somewhat shallow sylph who swaggers up to the unfortunate hero of the novel *à la mode*. So far from being unconventional and shallow, the boy is commonly conventional because he is secretive. He is much more sullen outside and much more morbid inside. Who then is this new Pantomime Boy, and where did she come from? In truth she comes out of a very old pantomime.

About three hundred years ago William Shakespeare, not knowing what to do with his characters, turned them out to play in the woods, let a girl masquerade as a boy and amused himself with speculating on the effect of feminine curiosity freed for an hour from feminine dignity. He did it very well, but he could do something else. And the popular romances of today cannot do anything else. Shakespeare took care to explain in the play itself that he did *not* think that life should be one prolonged picnic. Nor would he have thought that feminine life should be one prolonged piece of private theatricals. But Rosalind, who was then unconventional for an hour, is now the convention of an epoch. She was then on a holiday; she is now very hard-worked indeed. She has to act in every play, novel or short story, and always in the same old pert pose. Perhaps she is even afraid to be herself: certainly Celia is now afraid to be herself.

We should think it rather a bore if all tragic youths wore black cloaks and carried skulls in imitation of Hamlet, or all old men waved wands and clasped enormous books in imitation of Prospero. But we are almost as much tied to one type of girl in popular fiction today. And it is getting very tiresome. A huge human success is banking up for anybody bold enough to describe a quiet girl, a girl handicapped by good manners and a habit of minding her own business. Even a sulky girl would be a relief.

The moral is one we often draw; that the family is the real field for personality. All the best Shakespearian dramas are domestic dramas; even when mainly concerned with domestic murders. So far from freedom following on the decay of the family, what follows is uniformity. The Rosalinds become a sort of regiment; if it is a regiment of vivandières. They wear uniform of shingled hair and short skirts; and they seem to stand in a row like chorus girls. Not till we have got back within the four walls of the home shall we have any great tragedy or great comedy. The attempts to describe life in a Utopia of the future are alone enough to prove that there is nothing dramatic about an everlasting picnic.

Men and women must stand in some serious and lasting relation to each other for great passions and great problems to arise; and all this anarchy is as bad for art as it is for morals. Rosalind did not go into the wood to look for her freedom; she went into the wood to look for her father. And all the freedom; and even all the fun of the adventure really arises from that fact. For even an adventure must have an aim. Anyhow, the modern aimlessness has produced a condition in which we are so bored with Rosalind that we almost long for Lady Macbeth.

A Midsummer Night's Dream

The greatest of Shakespeare's comedies is also, from a certain point of view, the greatest of his plays. No one would maintain that it occupied this position in the matter of psychological study, if by psychological study we mean the study of individual characters in a play. No one would maintain that Puck was a character in the sense that Falstaff is a character, or that the critic stood awed before the psychology of Peaseblossom. But there is a sense in which the play is perhaps a greater triumph of psychology than *Hamlet* itself. It may well be questioned whether in any other literary work in the world is so vividly rendered a social and spiritual atmosphere. There is an atmosphere in *Hamlet*, for instance, a somewhat murky and even melodramatic one, but it is subordinate to the great character, and morally inferior to him; the darkness is only a background for the isolated star of intellect. But *A Midsummer Night's Dream* is a psychological study, not of a solitary man, but of a spirit that unites mankind. The six men may sit talking in an inn; they may not know each other's names or see each other's faces before or after, but night or wine or great stories, or some rich and branching discussion may make them all at one, if not absolutely with each other, at least with that invisible seventh man who is the harmony of all of them. That seventh man is the hero of *A Midsummer Night's Dream*.

A study of the play from a literary or philosophical point of view must therefore be founded upon some serious realization of what this atmosphere is. In a lecture upon *As You Like It*, Mr. Bernard Shaw made a suggestion which is an admirable example of his amazing ingenuity and of his one most interesting limitation. In maintaining that the light sentiment and optimism of the comedy were regarded by Shakespeare merely as the characteristics of a more or less cynical pot-boiler, he actually suggested that the title "As You Like It" was a taunting address to the public in disparagement of their taste and the dramatists's own work. If Mr. Bernard Shaw had conceived of Shakespeare as insisting that Ben Jonson should wear Jaeger underclothing or join the Blue Ribbon Army, or distribute little pamphlets for the non-payment of rates, he could scarcely have conceived anything more violently opposed to the whole spirit of Elizabethan comedy than the spiteful and priggish modernism of such a taunt. Shakespeare might make the fastidious and cultivated Hamlet, moving in his own melancholy and purely mental world, warn players against an over-indulgence towards the rabble. But the very soul and meaning of the great comedies is that of an uproarious communion, between the public and the play, a communion so chaotic that whole scenes of silliness and violence lead us almost to think that some of the "rowdies" from the pit have climbed over the footlights. The title "As You Like It" is, of course, an expression of utter carelessness, but it is not the bitter carelessness which Mr. Bernard Shaw fantastically reads into it; it is the godlike and inexhaustible carelessness of a happy man. And the simple proof of this is that there are scores of these genially taunting titles scattered through the whole of Elizabethan comedy. Is "As You Like It" a title demanding a dark and ironic explanation in a school of comedy which called its plays, "What You Will", "A Mad World, My Masters", "If It Be Not Good, the Devil Is In It", "The Devil is an Ass", "An Humorous Day's Mirth", and "A Midsummer Night's Dream"? Every one of these titles is flung at the head of the public as a drunken lord might fling a purse at his footman. Would Mr. Shaw maintain that "If It Be Not Good, the Devil Is In It", was the opposite of "As You Like It", and was a solemn invocation of the supernatural powers to testify to the care and perfection of the literary workmanship? The one explanation is as Elizabethan as the other.

Now in the reason for this modern and pedantic error lies the whole secret and difficulty of such plays as *A Midsummer Night's Dream*. The sentiment of such a play, so far as it can be summed up at all, can be summed up in one sentence. It is the mysticism of happiness. That is to say, it is the conception that as man lives upon a borderland he may find himself in the spiritual or supernatural atmosphere, not only through being profoundly sad or meditative, but by being extravagantly happy. The soul might be rapt out of the body in an agony of sorrow, or a trance of ecstasy; but it might also be rapt out of the body in a paroxysm of laughter. Sorrow we know can go beyond itself; so, according to Shakespeare, can pleasure go beyond itself and become something dangerous and unknown. And the reason that the logical and destructive modern school, of which Mr. Bernard Shaw is an example, does not grasp this purely exuberant nature of the comedies is simply that their logical and destructive attitude have rendered impossible the very experience of this preternatural exuberance. We cannot realize *As You Like It* if we are always considering it as we understand it. We cannot have *A Midsummer Night's Dream* if our one object in life is to keep ourselves awake with the black coffee of criticism. The whole question which is balanced, and balanced nobly and fairly, in *A Midsummer Night's Dream*, is whether the life of waking, or the life of the vision, is the real life, the *sine quâ non* of man. But it is difficult to see what superiority for the purpose of judging is possessed by people whose pride it is not to live the life of vision at all. At least it is questionable whether the Elizabethan did not know more about both worlds than the modern intellectual; it is not altogether improbable that Shakespeare would not only have had a clearer vision of the fairies, but would have shot very much straighter at a deer and netted much more money for his performances than a member of the Stage Society.

In pure poetry and the intoxication of words, Shakespeare never rose higher than he rises in this play. But in spite of this fact the supreme literary merit of *A Midsummer Night's Dream* is a merit of design. The amazing symmetry, the amazing artistic and moral beauty of that design, can be stated very briefly. The story opens in the sane and common world with the pleasant seriousness of very young lovers and very young friends. Then, as the figures advance into the tangled wood of young troubles and stolen happiness, a change and bewilderment begins to fall on them. They lose their way and their wits for they are in the heart of fairyland. Their words, their hungers, their very figures grow more and more dim and fantastic, like dreams within dreams, in the supernatural mist of Puck. Then the dream-fumes begin to clear, and characters and spectators begin to awaken together to the noise of horns and dogs and the clean and bracing morning. Theseus, the incarnation of a happy and generous rationalism, expounds in hackneyed and superb lines the sane view of such psychic experiences, pointing out with a reverent and sympathetic scepticism that all these fairies and spells are themselves but the emanations, the unconscious masterpieces, of man himself. The whole company falls back into a splendid human laughter. There is a rush for banqueting and private theatricals, and over all these things ripples one of those frivolous and inspired conversations in which every good saying seems to die in giving birth to another. If ever the son of man in his wanderings was at home and drinking by the fireside, he is at home in the house of Theseus. All the dreams have been forgotten, as a melancholy dream remembered throughout the morning might be forgotten in the human certainty of any other triumphant evening party; and so the play seems naturally ended. It began on the earth and it ends on the earth. Thus to round off the whole midsummer night's dream in an eclipse of daylight is an effect of genius. But of this comedy, as I have said, the mark is that genius goes beyond itself; and one touch is added which makes the play colossal. Theseus and his train retire with a crashing finale, full of humour and wisdom and things set right, and silence falls on the house. Then there comes a faint sound of little feet, and for a moment, as it were, the elves look into the house, asking which is the reality. "Suppose we are the realities and they the shadows." If that ending were acted properly any modern man would feel shaken to his marrow if he had to walk home from the theatre through a country lane.

It is a trite matter, of course, though in a general criticism a more or less indispensable one to comment upon another point of artistic perfection, the extraordinarily human and accurate manner in which the play catches the atmosphere of a dream. The chase and tangle and frustration of the incidents and personalities are well known to everyone who has dreamt of perpetually falling over precipices or perpetually missing trains. While following out clearly and legally the necessary narrative of the drama, the author contrives to include every one of the main peculiarities of the exasperating dream. Here is the pursuit of the man we cannot catch, the flight from the man we cannot see; here is the perpetual returning to the same place, here is the crazy alteration in the very objects of our desire, the substitution of one face for another face, the putting of the wrong souls in the wrong bodies, the fantastic disloyalties of the night, all this is as obvious as it is important. It is perhaps somewhat more worth remarking that there is about this confusion of comedy yet another essential characteristic of dreams. A dream can commonly be described as possessing an utter discordance of incident combined with a curious unity of mood; everything changes but the dreamer. It may begin with anything and end with anything, but if the dreamer is sad at the end he will be sad as if by prescience at the beginning; if he is cheerful at the beginning he will be cheerful if the stars fail. *A Midsummer Night's Dream* has in a most singular degree effected this difficult, this almost desperate subtlety. The events in the wandering wood are in themselves, and regarded as in broad daylight, not merely melancholy but bitterly cruel and ignominious. But yet by the spreading of an atmosphere as magic as the fog of Puck, Shakespeare contrives to make the whole matter mysteriously hilarious while it is palpably tragic, and mysteriously charitable, while it is in itself cynical. He contrives somehow to rob tragedy and treachery of their full sharpness, just as a toothache or a deadly danger from a tiger, or a precipice, is robbed of its sharpness in a pleasant dream. The creation of a brooding sentiment like this, a sentiment not merely independent of but actually opposed to the events, is a much greater triumph of art than the creation of the character of Othello.

It is difficult to approach critically so great a figure as that of Bottom the Weaver. He is greater and more mysterious than Hamlet, because the interest of such men as Bottom consists of a rich subconsciousness, and that of Hamlet in the comparatively superficial matter of a rich consciousness. And it is especially difficult in the present age which has become hag-ridden with the mere intellect. We are the victims of a curious confusion whereby being great is supposed to have something to do with being clever, as if there were the smallest reason to suppose that Achilles was clever, as if there were not on the contrary a great deal of internal evidence to indicate that he was next door to a fool. Greatness is a certain indescribable but perfectly familiar and palpable quality of size in the personality, of steadfastness, of strong flavour, of easy and natural self-expression. Such a man is as firm as a tree and as unique as a rhinoceros, and he might quite easily be as stupid as either of them. Fully as much as the great poet towers above the small poet the great fool towers above the small fool. We have all of us known rustics like Bottom the Weaver, men whose faces would be blank with idiocy if we tried for ten days to explain the meaning of the National Debt, but who are yet great men, akin to Sigurd and Hercules, heroes of the morning of the earth, because their words were their own words, their memories their own memories, and their vanity as large and simple as a great hill. We have all of us known friends in our own circle, men whom the intellectuals might justly describe as brainless, but whose presence in a room was like a fire roaring in the grate changing everything, lights and shadows and the air, whose entrances and exits were in some strange fashion events, whose point of view once expressed haunts and persuades the mind and almost intimidates it, whose manifest absurdity clings to the fancy like the beauty of first love, and whose follies are recounted like the legends of a paladin. These are great men, there are millions of them in the world, though very few perhaps in the House of Commons. It is not in the cold halls of cleverness where celebrities seem to be important that we should look for the great. An intellectual salon is merely a training-ground for one faculty, and is akin to a fencing class or a rifle corps. It is in our own homes and environments, from Croydon to St. John's Wood, in old nurses, and gentlemen with hobbies, and talkative spinsters and vast incomparable butlers, that we may feel the presence of that blood of the gods. And this creature so hard to describe, so easy to remember, the august and memorable fool, has never been so sumptuously painted as in the Bottom of *A Midsummer Night's Dream*.

Bottom has the supreme mark of this real greatness in that like the true saint or the true hero he only differs from humanity in being as it were more human than humanity. It is not true, as the idle materialists of today suggest, that compared to the majority of men the hero appears cold and dehumanized; it is the majority who appear cold and dehumanized in the presence of greatness. Bottom, like Don Quixote and Uncle Toby and Mr. Richard Swiveller and the rest of the Titans, has a huge and unfathomable weakness, his silliness is on a great scale, and when he blows his own trumpet it is like the trumpet of the Resurrection. The other rustics in the play accept his leadership not merely naturally but exuberantly;

they have to the full that primary and savage unselfishness, that uproarious abnegation which makes simple men take pleasure in falling short of a hero, that unquestionable element of basic human nature which has never been expressed, outside this play, so perfectly as in the incomparable chapter at the beginning of *Evan Harrington* in which the praises of The Great Mel are sung with a lyric energy by the tradesmen whom he has cheated. Twopenny sceptics write of the egoism of primal human nature; it is reserved for great men like Shakespeare and Meredith to detect and make vivid this rude and subconscious unselfishness which is older than self. They alone with their insatiable tolerance can perceive all the spiritual devotion in the soul of a snob. And it is this natural play between the rich simplicity of Bottom and the simple simplicity of his comrades which constitutes the unapproachable excellence of the farcical scenes in this play. Bottom's sensibility to literature is perfectly fiery and genuine, a great deal more genuine than that of a great many cultivated critics of literature—"the raging rocks and shivering shocks shall break the locks of prison gates, and Phibbus' car shall shine from far, and make and mar the foolish fates", is exceedingly good poetical diction with a real throb and swell in it, and if it is slightly and almost imperceptibly deficient in the matter of sense, it is certainly every bit as sensible as a good many other rhetorical speeches in Shakespeare put into the mouths of kings and lovers and even the spirits of the dead. If Bottom liked cant for its own sake the fact only constitutes another point of sympathy between him and his literary creator. But the style of the thing, though deliberately bombastic and ludicrous, is quite literary, the alliteration falls like wave upon wave, and the whole verse, like a billow mounts higher and higher before it crashes. There is nothing mean about this folly; nor is there in the whole realm of literature a figure so free from vulgarity. The man vitally base and foolish sings "The Honeysuckle and the Bee"; he does not rant about "raging rocks" and "the car of Phibbus". Dickens, who more perhaps than any modern man had the mental hospitality and the thoughtless wisdom of Shakespeare, perceived and expressed admirably the same truth. He perceived, that is to say, that quite indefensible idiots have very often a real sense of, and enthusiasm for letters. Mr. Micawber loved eloquence and poetry with his whole immortal soul; words and visionary pictures kept him alive in the absence of food and money, as they might have kept a saint fasting in a desert. Dick Swiveller did not make his inimitable quotations from Moore and Byron merely as flippant digressions. He made them because he loved a great school of poetry. The sincere love of books has nothing to do with cleverness or stupidity any more than any other sincere love. It is a quality of character, a freshness, a power of pleasure, a power of faith. A silly person may delight in reading masterpieces just as a silly person may delight in picking flowers. A fool may be in love with a poet as he may be in love with a woman. And the triumph of Bottom is that he loves rhetoric and his own taste in the arts, and this is all that can be achieved by Theseus, or for the matter of that by Cosimo di Medici. It is worth remarking as an extremely fine touch in the picture of Bottom that his literary taste is almost everywhere concerned with sound rather than sense. He begins the rehearsal with a boisterous readiness, "Thisby, the flowers of odious savours sweete." "Odours, odours," says Quince, in remonstrance, and the word is accepted in accordance with the cold and heavy rules which require an element of meaning in a poetical passage. But "Thisby, the flowers of odious savours sweete", Bottom's version, is an immeasurably finer and more resonant line. The "i" which he inserts is an inspiration of metricism.

There is another aspect of this great play which ought to be kept familiarly in the mind. Extravagant as is the masquerade of the story, it is a very perfect aesthetic harmony down to such *coup-de-maître* as the name of Bottom, or

the flower called Love-in-Idleness. In the whole matter it
may be said that there is one accidental discord; that is in
the name of Theseus, and the whole city of Athens in which
the events take place. Shakespeare's description of Athens in
A Midsummer Night's Dream is the best description of England that he or any one else ever wrote. Theseus is quite
obviously only an English squire, fond of hunting, kindly to
his tenants, hospitable with a certain flamboyant vanity. The
mechanics are English mechanics, talking to each other with
the queer formality of the poor. Above all, the fairies are
English; to compare them with the beautiful patrician spirits
of Irish legend, for instance, is suddenly to discover that we
have, after all, a folklore and a mythology, or had it at least
in Shakespeare's day. Robin Goodfellow, upsetting the old
women's ale, or pulling the stool from under them, has
nothing of the poignant Celtic beauty; his is the horse-play
of the invisible world. Perhaps it is some debased inheritance
of English life which makes American ghosts so fond of
quite undignified practical jokes. But this union of mystery
with farce is a note of the medieval English. The play is the
last glimpse of Merrie England, that distant but shining and
quite indubitable country. It would be difficult indeed to
define wherein lay the peculiar truth of the phrase "merrie
England", though some conception of it is quite necessary to
the comprehension of *A Midsummer Night's Dream*. In some
cases at least, it may be said to lie in this, that the English of
the Middle Ages and the Renaissance, unlike the England
of today, could conceive of the idea of a merry super-
naturalism. Amid all the great work of Puritanism the
damning indictment of it consists in one fact, that there was
one only of the fables of Christendom that it retained and
renewed, and that was the belief in witchcraft. It cast away
the generous and wholesome superstition, it approved only of
the morbid and the dangerous. In their treatment of the great
national fairy-tale of good and evil, the Puritans killed St.
George but carefully preserved the Dragon. And this seven-

teenth-century tradition of dealing with the psychic life still lies like a great shadow over England and America, so that if we glance at a novel about occultism we may be perfectly certain that it deals with sad or evil destiny. Whatever else we expect we certainly should never expect to find in it spirits such as those in *Aylwin* as inspirers of a tale of tomfoolery like the *Wrong Box* or *The Londoners*. That impossibility is the disappearance of "merrie England" and Robin Goodfellow. It was a land to us incredible, the land of a jolly occultism where the peasant cracked jokes with his patron saint, and only cursed the fairies good-humouredly, as he might curse a lazy servant. Shakespeare is English in everything, above all in his weaknesses. Just as London, one of the greatest cities in the world, shows more slums and hides more beauties than any other, so Shakespeare alone among the four giants of poetry is a careless writer, and lets us come upon his splendours by accident, as we come upon an old City church in the twist of a city street. He is English in nothing so much as in that noble cosmopolitan unconsciousness which makes him look eastward with the eyes of a child towards Athens or Verona. He loved to talk of the glory of foreign lands, but he talked of them with the tongue and unquenchable spirit of England. It is too much the custom of a later patriotism to reverse this method and talk of England from morning till night, but to talk of her in a manner totally un-English. Casualness, incongruities, and a certain fine absence of mind are in the temper of England; the unconscious man with the ass's head is no bad type of the people. Materialistic philosophers and mechanical politicians have certainly succeeded in some cases in giving him a greater unity. The only question is, to which animal has he been thus successfully conformed?

Part Four: Much Ado About Something

The Silver Goblets

It was reported that at the sumptuous performance of *Henry VIII* at His Majesty's Theatre, the urns and goblets of the banquet were specially wrought in real and solid silver and in the style of the sixteenth century. This bombastic literalism is at least very much the fashion in our modern theatricals. Mr. Vincent Crummles considered it a splendid piece of thoroughness on the part of an actor that he should black himself all over to perform Othello. But Mr. Crummles's ideal falls short of the theoretic thoroughness of the late Sir Herbert Tree, who would consider blacking oneself all over as comparatively a mere sham, compromise, and veneer. Sir Herbert Tree would, I suppose, send for a real Negro to act Othello, and perhaps for a real Jew to act Shylock—though that, in the present condition of the English stage, might possibly be easier. The strict principle of the silver goblets might be a little more arduous and unpleasant if applied, let us say, to *The Arabian Nights*, if the manager of His Majesty's Theatre presented *Aladdin*, and had to produce not one real Negro but a hundred real Negroes, carrying a hundred baskets of gigantic and genuine jewels. In the presence of this proposal even Sir Herbert might fall back on a simpler philosophy of the drama. For the principle in itself admits of no limit. If once it be allowed that what looks like silver behind the footlights is better also for really being silver, there seems no reason why the wildest developments should not ensue. The priests in *Henry VIII* might be specially ordained in the greenroom before they come on. Nay, if it comes to that, the head of Buckingham might easily be cut off, as in the glad old days lamented by Swinburne, before the coming of an emasculate mysticism removed real death from the arena. We might re-establish the goriness as well as the gorgeousness of the amphitheatre. If real wine-cups, why not real wine? If real wine, why not real blood?

Nor is this an illegitimate or irrelevant deduction. This and a hundred other fantasies might follow if once we admit the first principle that we need to realize on the stage not merely the beauty of silver, but the value of silver. Shakespeare's famous phrase that art should hold the mirror up to nature is always taken as wholly realistic; but it is really idealistic and symbolic—at least, compared with the realism of His Majesty's. Art is a mirror not because it is the same as the object, but because it is different. A mirror selects as much as art selects; it gives the light of flames, but not their heat; the colour of flowers, but not their fragrance; the faces of women, but not their voices; the proportions of stockbrokers, but not their solidity. A mirror is a vision of things, not a working model of them. And the silver seen in a mirror is not for sale.

But the results of the thing in practice are worse than its wildest results in history. This Arabian extravagance in the furniture and decoration of a play has one very practical disadvantage—that it narrows the number of experiments, confines them to a small and wealthy class, and makes those which are made exceptional, erratic, and unrepresentative of any general dramatic activity. One or two insanely expensive works prove nothing about the general state of art in a country. To take the parallel of a performance somewhat less dignified, perhaps, than Sir Herbert Tree's, there has lately been in America an exhibition not unanalogous to a conflict in the arena, and one for which a real Negro actually was procured by the management. The Negro happened to beat the white man, and both before and after this event people went about wildly talking of "The White Man's champion" and "the representative of the Black Race". All black men were supposed to have triumphed over all white men in a sort of mysterious Armageddon because one specialist met another specialist and tapped his claret or punched him in the bread-basket.

Now the fact is, of course, that these two prize-fighters were so specially picked and trained—the business of producing such men is so elaborate, artificial and expensive—that the result proves nothing whatever about the general condition of white men or black. If you go in for heroes or monsters it is obvious that they may be born anywhere. If you took the two tallest men on earth, one might be born in Korea and the other in Camberwell, but this would not make Camberwell a land of giants inheriting the blood of Anak. If you took the two thinnest men in the world, one might be a Parisian and the other a Red Indian. And if you take the two most scientifically developed pugilists, it is not surprising that one of them should happen to be white and the other black. Experiments of so special and profuse a kind have the character of monstrosities, like black tulips or blue roses. It is absurd to make them representative of races and causes that they do not represent. You might as well say that the Bearded Lady at a fair represents the masculine advance of modern woman; or that all Europe was shaking under the banded armies of Asia, because of the co-operation of the Siamese Twins.

So the plutocratic tendency of such performances as *Henry VIII* is to prevent rather than to embody any movement of historical or theatrical imagination. If the standard of expenditure is set so high by custom, the number of competitors must necessarily be small, and will probably be of a restricted and unsatisfactory type. Instead of English history and English literature being as cheap as silver paper, they will be as dear as silver plate. The national culture, instead of being spread out everywhere like gold leaf, will be hardened into a few costly lumps of gold—and kept in very few pockets. The modern world is full of things that are theoretically open and popular, but practically private and even corrupt. In theory any tinker can be chosen to speak for his fellow-citizens among the English Commons. In practice he may have to spend a thousand pounds on getting elected—a sum which many tinkers do not happen to have to spare. In theory it ought to be possible for any moderately successful actor with a sincere and interesting conception of Wolsey to put that conception on the stage. In practice it looks as if he would have to ask himself, not whether he was as clever as Wolsey, but whether he was as rich. He has to reflect, not whether he can enter into Wolsey's soul, but whether he can pay Wolsey's servants, purchase Wolsey's plate, and own Wolsey's palaces.

Now people with Wolsey's money and people with Wolsey's mind are both rare; and even with him the mind came before the money. The chance of their being combined a second time is manifestly small and decreasing. The result will obviously be that thousands and millions may be spent on a theatrical misfit, and inappropriate and unconvincing impersonation; and all the time there may be a man outside who could have put on a red dressing-gown and made us feel in the presence of the most terrible of the Tudor statesmen. The modern method is to sell Shakespeare for thirty pieces of silver.

Poor Old Shakespeare

Shakespeare, we are too frequently informed, said that a rose by any other name would smell as sweet; it would be more correct to say that Shakespeare said that Miss Juliet Capulet said it, in a rather distracted moment in a romantic play. It would cause more surprise to announce that Shakespeare said, "I am determined to be a villain"; because he said that Richard the Third said it, in a rather melodramatic play. But anyhow the maxim and the metaphor have clung to men's memories and produced curious results. Some gardeners, it would seem, supposed that because the rose would be as sweet with any other name, therefore the name would be as sweet with any other flower; and merely turned "rose-tree" into Greek and applied it to a rhododendron. It is rather typical of the way in which science sometimes tells lies in Greek, which would be too obvious in English. Other philosophers, of the realistic or cynical school, apply the maxim in a still more curious way; as meaning that because one rose has the name of a cabbage-rose, therefore a rose is the same as a cabbage. But most sensible people know the real sense of the phrase; that the world is too prone to look at the title rather than the thing; at the label rather than the bottle, or the bottle rather than the wine. In this sense we can heartily agree with Miss Capulet, however distracted. Having to choose between the two, a man would be less than wise if he refused to drink good wine out of the bottle and were left merely licking the gum off the label.

So it is doubtless with roses in real life; but not entirely so in real literature. If a rose-grower had an eccentric benefactor, who stipulated that the word "rose" should never be uttered; that the word "hogswash" or "pignut" should be invariably substituted, but on these conditions undertook to smother him in masses of the most gorgeous and fragrant blooms of innumerable rose-gardens, the recipient would doubtless be wise to prefer the thing to the word. But it does not follow that it does not matter what we do with the word. In the heritage of poetry, which is a great part of civilization, the word is almost as valuable as the thing; indeed the word is already part of the thing. Even Juliet shrank from actually suggesting any other name, and "hogswash" would have a good deal thrown her out of her own stride. It is not true that a love song like "My love is like the red red pignut" would leap to the lips of every lover, even if a footnote explained that the term was identical with the botanical Latin name for the rose. Even for anyone accepting the convention, the opening line, "It was hogswash hogswash all the way", would never recapture the first fine careless rapture of Browning's line. In short, the name is not the thing; but the name is very far from being a mere number or sign for the thing. Man and Nature have so long reacted on each other, that I strongly suspect that kingcups or hyacinths do actually look nobler to us because of their ancient and noble names.

To forget this is to forget the very meaning of culture, which should run parallel to horticulture. And some moderns of the hogswash and pignut school of poetry, seem likely to forget it. The revolt against culture is often the last fashion of the cultured. But above all, it is very unfair to poor old Shakespeare. If ever there was a man who did not agree with Juliet's distracted remark, in its realistic sense, it was he. If ever a man could smell mere words, as if they were flowers, and do without the flowers, it was he. Heaven knows why the world has remembered this one chance phrase of Juliet, and forgotten a thousand gorgeous and odorous phrases that rise almost like stupefying fumes. "Not poppy nor mandragora. . . ." Surely everybody knows those intoxicant ingredients. But I gravely doubt whether Shakespeare even knew what mandragora looked like.

On Stage Costume (Part I)

While watching the other evening a very well-managed reproduction of *A Midsummer Night's Dream*, I had the sudden conviction that the play would be much better if it were acted in modern costume, or, at any rate, in English costume. We all remember hearing in our boyhood about the absurd conventionality of Garrick and Mrs. Siddons, when he acted Macbeth in a tie-wig and a tail-coat and she acted Lady Macbeth in a crinoline as big and stiff as a cartwheel. This has always been talked of as a piece of comic ignorance or impudent modernity; as if Rosalind appeared in rational dress with a bicycle; as if Portia appeared with a horsehair wig and side whiskers. But I am not so sure that the great men and women who founded the English stage in the eighteenth century were quite such fools as they looked; especially as they looked to the romantic historians and eager archaeologists of the nineteenth century. I have a queer suspicion that Garrick and Siddons knew nearly as much about dressing as they did about acting.

One distinction can at least be called obvious. Garrick did not care much for the historical costume of Macbeth; but he cared as much as Shakespeare did. He did not know much about that prehistoric and partly mythical Celtic chief; but he knew more than Shakespeare; and he could not conceivably have cared less. Now the Victorian age was honestly interested in the dark and epic origins of Europe; was honestly interested in Picts and Scots, in Celts and Saxons; in the blind drift of the races and the blind drive of the religions. Ossian and the Arthurian revival had interested people in distant dark-headed men who probably never existed. Freeman, Carlyle, and the other Teutonists had interested them in distant fair-headed men who almost certainly never existed. Pusey and Pugin and the first High Churchmen had interested them in shaven-headed men, dark or fair, men who did undoubtedly exist, but whose real merits and defects would have startled their modern admirers very considerably. Under these circumstances it is not strange that our age should have felt a curiosity about the solid but mysterious Macbeth of the Dark Ages. But all this does not alter the ultimate fact: that the only Macbeth that mankind will ever care about is the Macbeth of Shakespeare, and not the Macbeth of history. When England was romantic it was interested in Macbeth's kilt and claymore. In the same way, if England becomes a Republic, it will be specially interested in the Republicans in *Julius Caesar*. If England becomes Roman Catholic, it will be specially interested in the theory of chastity in *Measure for Measure*. But being interested in these things will never be the same as being interested in Shakespeare. And for a man interested in Shakespeare, a man merely concerned about what Shakespeare meant, a Macbeth in powdered hair and knee-breeches is perfectly satisfactory. For Macbeth, as Shakespeare shows him, is much more like a man in knee-breeches than a man in a kilt. His subtle hesitations and his suicidal impenitence belong to the bottomless speculations of a highly civilized society. The "Out, out, brief candle" is far more appropriate to the last wax taper after a ball of powder and patches than to the smoky but sustained fires in iron baskets which probably flared and smouldered over the swift crimes of the eleventh century. The real Macbeth probably killed Duncan with the nearest weapon, and then confessed it to the nearest priest. Certainly, he may never have had any such doubts about the normal satisfaction of being alive. However regrettably negligent of the importance of Duncan's life, he had, I fancy, few philosophical troubles about the importance of his own. The men of the Dark Ages were all optimists, as all children and all animals are. The madness of Shakespeare's

Macbeth goes along with candles and silk stockings. That madness only appears in the age of reason.

So far, then, from Garrick's anachronism being despised, I should like to see it imitated. Shakespeare got the tale of Theseus from Athens, as he got the tale of Macbeth from Scotland; and having reluctantly seen the names of those two countries in the record, I am convinced that he never gave them another thought. Macbeth is not a Scotchman; he is a man. But Theseus is not only not an Athenian; he is actually and unmistakably an Englishman. He is the Super-Squire; the best version of the English country gentleman; better than Wardel in *Pickwick*. The Duke of Athens is a duke (that is, a dook), but not of Athens. That free city is thousands of miles away.

If Theseus came on the stage in gaiters or a shooting-jacket, if Bottom the Weaver wore a smock-frock, if Hermia and Helena were dressed as two modern English schoolgirls, we should not be departing from Shakespeare, but rather returning to him. The cold classical draperies (of which he probably never dreamed, but with which we drape Aegisthus or Hippolyta) are not only a nuisance, but a falsehood. They misrepresent the whole meaning of the play. For the meaning of the play is that the little things of life as well as the great things stray on the borderland of the unknown. That as a man may fall among devils for a morbid crime, or fall among angels for a small piece of piety or pity, so also he may fall among fairies through an amiable flirtation or a fanciful jealousy. The fact that a back door opens into elfland is all the more reason for keeping the foreground familiar, and even prosaic. For even the fairies are very neighbourly and fire-light fairies; therefore the human beings ought to be very human in order to effect the fantastic contrast. And in Shakespeare they are very human. Hermia the vixen and Helena the maypole are obviously only two excitable and quite modern girls. Hippolyta has never been an Amazon; she may perhaps have once been a Suffragette. Theseus is a gentleman, a thing entirely different from a Greek oligarch. That golden good-nature which employs culture itself to excuse the clumsiness of the uncultured is a thing quite peculiar to those lazier Christian countries where the Christian gentleman has been evolved:

> For nothing in this world can be amiss
> When simpleness and duty tender it.

Or again, in that noble scrap of sceptical magnanimity:

> The best in this kind are but shadows; and the
> worst are no worse if imagination amend them.

These are obviously the easy and reconciling comments of some kindly but cultivated squire, who will not pretend to his guests that the play is good, but who will not let the actors see that he thinks it bad. But this is certainly not the way in which an Athenian Tory like Aristophanes would have talked about a bad play.

But as the play is dressed and acted at present, the whole idea is inverted. We do not seem to creep out of a human house into a natural wood and there find the superhuman and supernatural. The mortals, in their tunics and togas, seem more distant from us than the fairies in their hoods and peaked caps. It is an anticlimax to meet the English elves when we have already encountered the Greek gods. The same mistake, oddly enough, was made in the only modern play worth mentioning in the same street with *A Midsummer Night's Dream*, *Peter Pan*. Sir James Barrie ought to have left out the fairy dog who puts the children to bed. If children had such dogs as that they would never wish to go to fairy-land.

This fault or falsity in *Peter Pan* is, of course, repeated in the strange and ungainly incident of the father being chained up in the dog's kennel. Here, indeed, it is much worse: for the manlike dog was pretty and touching; the doglike man was ignominious and repulsive. But the fallacy is the same; it is the fallacy that weakens the otherwise triumphant poetry and wit of Sir James Barrie's play; and weakens all our treatment of fairy plays at present. Fairyland is a place of positive realities, plain laws, and a decisive story. The actors of *A Midsummer Night's Dream* seemed to think that the play was meant to be chaotic. The clowns thought they must be always clowning. But in reality it is the solemnity—nay, the conscientiousness—of the yokels that is akin to the mystery of the landscape and the tale.

On Stage Costume (Part II)

The Drury Lane performance of *A Midsummer Night's Dream*, which almost avowedly turned it into a Christmas pantomime, did not, in my opinion, fail thereby in respect for its great traditional and almost religious beauty; for there can be nothing more Christian than Christmas and nothing more ancient that pantomime. Especially do I rejoice in the fact that the clowns really were clowns, in the sense of clowns and pantaloons. It seems to me quite as bad art to play Bottom in a quiet realistic way as to play Hamlet in a vulgar theatrical way. I know not if any dramatic critic has expressed the joy which one spectator at least felt in the impersonation of the Wall; certainly the wittiest partition that ever I heard discourse, though the discourse consisted almost entirely of a laugh. But I have no intention of trespassing on the province of any such dramatic critics. I refer to the particular performance for the moment because it raises, as do all such performances, one particular question of historical and artistic setting. The bridal of Theseus and Hippolita was set in the stiff but strongly coloured framework of archaic Greek art with the red clay and black profiles of Greek vases; and for the spectacular and pantomime purpose the effect was very fine. But we all know in reading the play that Theseus is no more than an archaic Achaean chief than Hamlet is a barbaric Danish Viking. If Theseus, like Snug the Joiner, could be induced to name his name and tell them plainly who he is, it would soon be apparent that he, Theseus, is not Theseus but Southampton or Essex, or some genial gentleman of Elizabethan culture and exceedingly English good nature. His making the best of a bad play is something I recognize as something more unmistakable than St. George's Cross. I do not think that national virtue is the one thing needful, but I think it very national. There may or may not have been a Greek Theseus; but I cannot imagine a French Theseus—still less an Irish one.

But I mention the matter here for another reason. There is a certain maxim that nearly everybody now repeats and I am disposed to dispute. It is of the sort not very easy to dispute; because it is not yet a proverb, though it is rapidly becoming a platitude. It is at that precise stage at which everybody says it, yet everybody thinks he is alone in saying it. It is said for the thousandth time with an irritating freshness, as if it were said for the first time. It is to this effect; that we only think our own age vulgar and past ages romantic because people in past ages did the same. They also thought their own clothes comic or commonplace, and the clothes of their grand-fathers dignified and distinguished. Old clothes are only beautiful as distant hills are blue—with distance. Thus Mr. Kipling describes the prehistoric men as saying that Romance went with bone and flint and could not survive metals and fire. Thus many have said that my praise of the Guilds is only the recurrent retrospective romance of a past Golden Age. It is suggested that men always think the present pro-saic and only the past poetical.

I venture to doubt it. And I will test it by this plain and practical test of theatrical costume. Suppose I suggested that *Hamlet*, let us say, should be acted seriously in modern costume. It might be quite interesting—if occasionally rather amusing. It would begin, I suppose, with a sentinel in a busby—like the sentry in *Iolanthe*. Then Horatio would come on in evening dress, smoking a cigarette. And so on through-out, up to the last catastrophic scene when the Queen takes the tabloid and the king is shot with the automatic. Hamlet was in many ways very modern; and many of his sceptical meditations would sound very suitable to evening dress and a cigarette. Nevertheless, it would be impossible to prevent it seeming like a burlesque. Yet Garrick acted Macbeth in powdered hair and a coat and breeches of his own period; and it did not seem like a burlesque. Why? The simple reason is, I believe, that men in former ages did *not* have the contempt for their own costume that we have today. They did *not* think knee-breeches absurd, as we think trousers absurd. They did *not* think a triangular hat a joke, as we think a top-hat a joke. It is a modern custom to despise modern costume.

It is clear, I think, that Shakespeare thought of his most dignified figures in Elizabethan or Jacobean fashions. He saw Hamlet with a beard; I suspect he saw him with a ruff. The mortal combat is not the less heroic because Osric can gush over the new pattern of the swords. From the innumerable incidental allusions to sixteenth-century custom and costume in Shakespearian plays, I am convinced that the poet thought in terms of his own time, even if it was, so to speak, when he was thinking without thinking. And nothing is so great in Shakespeare as those abrupt and unexpected bursts of thoughtless thought. But at least he cannot have felt the details altogher incongruous with the design. I take it that for various reasons such details of daily life were really not felt as ignominious or farcical. Of course, there really is in all cases, and was in his case, a certain moderate and normal tendency to regard the remote past as something mystical and imaginative. But it is one thing to do that and another to regard your own hat as merely a bad joke or a blot on the Forest of Arden.

The Merits of Shakespeare's Plots

I see that Mr. John M. Robertson has written a book about the problem of "Hamlet", round which the critics still revolve with all the irresolution of which they accuse the hero. I have not read Mr. Robertson's book and am thus inhibited by a fine fantastic scruple from reviewing it. But I gather from one of the shrewdest and sanest of critics, Mr. J. C. Squire, that it explains the inconsistencies of the play as mainly the rugged remains of the old romances or chronicles. It may be suggested that in truth a hero is made human when he is made inconsistent. This is true; but the explanation is at least a great improvement on the insane seriousness of the German psychologists. They talked of Hamlet not merely as a human character but as a historical character. They talked as if he had secrets not only hidden from Shakespeare's readers, but hidden from Shakespeare. This is madness; it is merely staring at a portrait till you think it is alive. It is as if they undertook to tell me the real truth about the private life of Oberon.

Moreover, the case of Hamlet does happen to be one in which Mr. Robertson's theory seems relatively right. I should deny any inconsistency in a dreamer doing sudden things like stabbing Polonius; they are just the sort of things a dreamer would do. But it is true that some things out of the old story seem harsh and irrelevant and it is truer still that the old story contains less than usual of the soul of the new story. I say "less than usual", for I should like to point out that the general rule is rather the other way. Mr. Robertson's thesis may be true of *Hamlet*, but it is not so true of Shakespeare.

Or course, much can be said by this time both for and against the national poet. But if it be hopeless to denounce

Shakespeare, it may appear almost as impertinent to defend him. And yet there is one point on which he has never been defended. And it is one on which I think he should not only be defended but admired. If I were a Shakespearian student or any kind of student (the improbability of which prospect words wholly fail me to express), I should specialize in the part of Shakespeare that is certainly not Shakespeare. I mean I should plead for the merit of Shakespeare's plots; all the more because they were somebody else's plots. In short, I should say a word for the poet's taste; if only his taste in theft. It is the fashion to abuse Shakespeare as a critic, if only to exalt him the more as a creator. It is the fashion to say that he built on a foundation of mere rubbish and that this lifts to a greater glory the cloud-capped pinnacles he reared upon it. I am not sure that it is such pure praise for a practical architect to say that he was totally indifferent to the basement and cellars, and interested exclusively in the roof and chimneypots. But, anyhow, I am sure that Shakespeare did not forget the foundation or despise the basement or the cellars.

Shakespeare *enjoyed* the old stories. He enjoyed them as tales are intended to be enjoyed. He liked reading them as a man of imagination and intelligence today likes reading a good adventure story, or still more a good detective story. This is the one possibility that the Shakespearian critics never seem to entertain. Probably they are not simple enough and therefore not imaginative enough to know what that enjoyment is. They cannot read an adventure story or indeed any story. For instance, nearly all the critics apologize, in a prim and priggish manner, for the tale on which turns the Trial Scene in *The Merchant of Venice*. They explain that poor Shakespeare had taken a barbarous old story and had to make the best of it. As a matter of fact, he had taken an uncommonly good story, one of the best that he could possibly have had to make the best of. It is a clear, pointed and practical parable against usury. The idea of a man forfeiting part of his body (it might have been an arm or leg) is

a highly philosophical satire on unlimited recovery of ruinous
debts. The idea is embodied in all those truly Christian laws
about wainage and livelihood which were the glory of the
Middle Ages. The story is excellent, simply as an anecdote
working up to a climax and ending in an unexpected retort.
And the end is a truth and not merely a trick. You do prove
the falsity of pedantic logic by a *reductio ad absurdum*.

While we have had masses of learned work about the
Shakespearian origins, we have had very little about the
Shakespearian origin. I mean we have had very little on the
main matter of his human and natural inheritance of the
whole civilization of Christendom from which he came. It is
a commonplace that Shakespeare was a result of the
Renaissance; but the Renaissance itself was a result of the
Middle Ages; nor was it by any means m~~~~~ ~st
the Middle A~~~ ~h
Shakespear ~e
than he w: e
stronger fo ~
patriotism i: ~
world; and S
very passage
out ceasing t(
sort called a n
days of Elizab
It is not abou

      As i~
      Of th

That note v
modern world;
cared to notice
have brought u: , ~~~ the footsteps of
our fathers; and ~~~ vision of John of Gaunt was fulfilled in
the hour when a great English soldier entered Jerusalem on
foot.

The Ideal Detective Story

There has been some renewal of debate on the problem of the problem story; in the social sense of the detective story, but there is one aspect which is almost inevitably left out. That tales of this type are generally slight, sensational and in some ways superficial, I know better than most people; for I have written them myself. If I say there is in the abstract something which may be called the Ideal Detective Story, I do not mean that I can write it. I call it the Ideal Detective Story because I cannot write it. Anyhow, I do think that such a story, while it must be sensational, need not be superficial. In theory, though not commonly in practice, it is possible to write a subtle and creative novel, of deep philosophy and delicate psychology, and yet cast it in the form of a sensational shocker.

For the point is very largely a matter of the order in which things are mentioned, rather than of the nature of the things themselves. The essence of a mystery tale is that we are suddenly confronted with a truth, which we have never suspected and yet can see to be true. There is no reason, in logic, why this truth should not be a profound and convincing one, as much as a shallow and conventional one. There is no reason why the hero who turns out to be a villain, or the villain who turns out to be a hero, should not be a study in the living subtleties and complexities of human character, on a level with the first figures in human fiction. It is only an accident of the actual origin of these detective novels, that the interest of the inconsistency commonly goes no further than that of a demure governess being a poisoner or a dull and colourless clerk being filled with a devouring and demoniac hatred. There are inconsistencies in human nature of a much higher and more mysterious order, and there is really no reason why they should not be presented in the particular way that causes the shock of a detective story. It is, as I have said, very largely a matter of the mere order of events. The side of the character that cannot be connected with the crime has to be presented first; the crime has to be presented next as something in complete contrast with it; and the psychological reconciliation of the two must come after that, in the place where the common or garden detective explains that he was led to the truth by the stump of a cigar left on the lawn or the spot of red ink on the blotting-pad in the boudoir. But there is nothing in the nature of things to prevent the explanation, when it does come, being as convincing to a psychologist as to a policeman.

Take Shakespeare, for instance; he has created two or three extremely amiable and sympathetic murderers. Only we can watch their amiability slowly and gently merging into murder. Othello is an affectionate husband who assassinates his wife out of sheer affection, so to speak, but as we know the story from the first, we can see the connection and accept the contradiction. But suppose the story opened with Desdemona found dead, Iago or Cassio suspected, and Othello the very last person likely to be suspected. In that case *Othello* would be a detective story. But it might be a true detective story; that is, one consistent with the true character of the hero when he finally tells the truth. Hamlet again is a most lovable and even peaceable person, as a rule; and we pardon the nervous and slightly irritable gesture which happens to have the result of sticking an old fool like a pig behind a curtain. But suppose the curtain rises on the corpse of Polonius, and Rosencrantz and Guildenstern discuss the suspicion that has immediately fallen on the First Player, an immoral actor accustomed to killing people on the stage; while Horatio or some shrewd character suspects another crime of Claudius or the reckless and unscrupulous Laertes. Then *Hamlet* would be a shocker, and the guilt of Hamlet would be a shock. But it might be a shock of truth; and it is not only sex novels that are shocking. These Shakespearian characters would be none the less coherent and all of a piece, because we brought the opposite ends of the character together, and tied them into a knot. The story of Othello might be published with a lurid wrapper as "The Pillow Murder Case". But it might still be the same case; a serious case, and a convincing case. The death of Polonius might appear on the bookstalls as "The Vanishing Rat Mystery" and be in form like an ordinary detective story. Yet it might be the Ideal Detective Story.

Nor need there be anything vulgar in the violent and abrupt transition that is the essential of such a tale. The inconsistencies of human nature are indeed terrible and heart-shaking things to be named with the same note of crisis as the hour of death and the day of judgment. They are not all fine shades, but some of them very fearful shadows, made by the primal contrast of darkness and light. Both the crimes and the confessions can be as catastrophic as lightning. Indeed the Ideal Detective Story might do some good if it brought men back to understand that the world is not all curves; but that there are some things that are as jagged as the lightning flash or as straight as the sword.

The Phoenix and the Turtle

How many of my highly cultured readers have really grasped,
assimilated and made their own the poem called "The
Phoenix and the Turtle"? I feel as if I were offering a prize
in the newspapers for some sort of success with a crossword
puzzle; but I can assure the reader that Torquemada never
produced anything within a thousand miles of the Turtle
and his mystical colleague. Much of the modern public will
be divided between those who say, "Of course we know
our Shakespeare," and those who have entirely forgotten
that Shakespeare ever wrote anything of the sort. And,
indeed, the first group is wrong and the second group is right.
Shakespeare never did write anything of the sort, so far as I
know, except in this one extraordinary example. On the
other hand, we may be fairly certain that those who say they
know their Shakespeare do not know their Shakespeare. If
they did they would not fall into the fallacy of supposing that
he was theirs. In all this common cultivated acquaintance
with the classics there is a certain unconscious trick of omis-
sion for which we must always allow. There is even a sort of
terrible irony in Matthew Arnold's phrase that culture consists of knowing "the best that has been said and thought".
It is only too true that the knowledge of Shakespeare generally means the knowledge of the best things in Shakespeare.
Or, at least, of the things which those who were thought the
best critics thought were the best things. But there are many
more marvellous fish in that great sea than ever came out of
it. When people say they know their Shakespeare, they
generally mean that they know somebody else's Shakespeare;
especially the actor's Shakespeare, or the actor-manager's
Shakespeare, or the highly modern producer's Shakespeare,

or, what is worst of all, the Shakespeare critic's Shakespeare.

It is the same with all the great creations that are stared at like monuments, rather than quarried in like mines. I read a newspaper article the other day in which a man said that he knew the message of the Gospel was quite simple, because he had heard it at his mother's knee. It did not seem to occur to him that his mother might have been a person of some common sense and that she probably read to him the passages that really are simple enough to be suitable to a child. It seems probable that she was sane enough to tell him of the Good Shepherd who goes after the lost sheep; or the welcome to the prodigal returning home; or the love of Christ for all little children. It seems improbable that she asked a child to understand what is meant by the Unjust Steward; or the Eunuchs of the Kingdom of Heaven; or the command to hate father and mother for the Kingdom of God; or the bringing of a sword into the world; or the dark enigma of Judas. Now, most educated people have exactly that memory of an expurgated Shakespeare; as they have of an expurgated Bible. They remember the things that have been theatrically presented to them; because they are theatrical. They remember the things that are quite obviously edifying, in the sense of moralizing, because they have been imposed upon them. But there are a thousand things in Shakespeare which they have never even tried to understand; and this is something which I respectfully doubt whether they would understand even if they tried.

People actually found cryptograms in Shakespeare; but there is nothing so very cryptic about a cryptogram. It is merely a sort of spelling game, by which a rather crude and clumsy series of words can somehow be traced through the thick of much more important and intelligent and beautiful words. ... We can prove the impossibility of a cryptogram by the existence of so many cryptograms. The more often it is done, the more impossible it is to do. There have been about ten alternative explanations of the authorship of the plays, founded on a long recurrent scheme running through the plays. I have never seen one real explanation of the short poem called "The Phoenix and the Turtle". I mean I have never seen any in the ordinary literary textbooks. Or, again, I have read all my life about the obscurity of certain writers; of how Browning baffles the reader, or even Meredith is sometimes verbally evasive. But I was never baffled by Browning or Meredith, even in my boyhood; and I am pretty completely baffled by "The Phoenix and the Turtle". Yet, strangely enough, it is never mentioned among these other and milder examples of popular misunderstanding. I come back with some gloom to the inference: not that nobody has understood it, but that nobody has read it.

Of course, I would not be arrogant. There may be others who grasp it at a glance; whose common conversation at breakfast consists of lines like these—

> Reason, in itself confounded,
> Saw division grow together,
> To themselves yet either neither,
> Simple were so well compounded
> That it cried, How true a twain
> Seemeth this concordant one!

But I have not come across any of them among the public Shakespearian critics. Shakespeare did really wish to leave behind him one real cryptogram; not a silly alphabetical cypher to say that he was Francis Bacon or Queen Elizabeth, or the Earl of Southampton; but something to say that he was the Shakespeare whom we shall never know. As if he had been suddenly alarmed at the horrid notion that he had really unlocked his heart with the key of the Sonnets, as Wordsworth suggested; and had then resolved to leave behind him a casket that no key can unlock.

I do not set up to be a student of Shakespeare, still less of Shakespeariana. . . . The only serious and convincing note on it I happen to have read is in the Comtesse de Chambrun's

remarkable reconstruction called, "My Shakespeare, Rise!"
M. André Maurois writes a most interesting preface to this
most interesting book. Himself detached from the debates on
which it turns, he is only linked with Mme de Chambrun by
his interest in English literature; but he pays a just tribute to
the learning which she applies to that literature. Her theory
is, broadly speaking, that the motive that made Shakespeare
thus cryptic was largely politic; and that the whole mystery
was connected with contemporary politics. She has set out in
several books her reasons for believing that Shakespeare
belonged to the party, at once of revolt and reaction; which
was specially bent on breaking the power and policy of Cecil
and his group; a group which more or less included Bacon. It
is curious that Bacon and Shakespeare, who have actually
been lumped together as partners, or even identified as an
alias and an *alter ego*, were (according to this theory) so far
from working together in private life, actually working
against each other in public life. This particular movement
found its final issue and failure, I suppose, in the rebellion of
Essex, which was certainly against Cecil on the political side,
though some have disputed its purpose on the religious
side. Essex may have courted some of the Puritans; his friend
Southampton was certainly one of the Papists; and this book
explains the mysterious lament as a dirge for the old régime:
"Truth may seem but cannot be; Beauty brag, but 'tis not
she." Certainly that is what a man might well say, who felt
hostile to a new world.

Shakespeare *v*. Milton

It is not unnatural that there should be a certain vagueness about the personal celebration of Shakespeare in his own personal place of residence. In the very highest artist there is always a disdain of art. Shakespeare left his manuscripts loose all over the place as if they were old envelopes; and it may seem curious, and even exasperating, that the learned world should think so much of some pieces of paper of which their author thought so little. But even in this queer and casual aloofness Shakespeare is very satisfactorily typical of the English nation. It has been said that England created an empire in a fit of absence of mind; it is quite certain that William Shakespeare created a drama in a fit of absence of mind. All that is best in England is expressed in the fact that Shakespeare has no biography; which means that he had a very jolly life. All that is good in England is always all the better because it comes unexpectedly, because it comes unreasonably, as an English town comes suddenly at a twist of an English road. . . . Even Shakespeare was a splendid accident and little as we know of his life, he seems always to have behaved like one.

Nearly all Englishmen are either Shakespearians or Miltonians. I do not mean that they admire one more than another; because everyone in his senses must admire both of them infinitely. I mean that each represents something in the make-up of England; and that the two things are so antagonistic that it is really impossible not to be secretly on one side or the other. The difference, in so far as it concerns the two men, can be expressed in all sorts of ways; but every way taken by itself is inadequate. Shakespeare represents the Catholic, Milton the Protestant.

... I respectfully decline to explain in a space like this exactly why I feel one religion in one author and another religion in another. I think the remarks of Aristotle somewhat too compressed to be clearly understood; still I can understand that Aristotle was a pagan. ... These impressions are hard to explain, because they are impressions of everything. But here, at least, is one way of putting the difference between the religions of Shakespeare and Milton. Milton is possessed with what is, I suppose, the first and finest idea of Protestantism—the idea of the individual soul actually testing and tasting all the truth there is, and calling that truth which it has not tested or tasted truth of a less valuable and vivid kind. But Shakespeare is possessed through and through with the feeling which is the first and finest idea of Catholicism— that truth exists whether we like it or not, and that it is for us to accommodate ourselves to it. Milton, with a splendid infallibility and a splendid intolerance, sets out to describe how things actually are to be explained; he has seen it in a vision—

> That to the height of this great argument
> I may assert eternal Providence,
> And justify the ways of God to men.

But when Shakespeare speaks of the divine truth, it is always as something from which he himself may have fallen away, something that he himself may have forgotten—

> O ... that the Everlasting had not fix'd
> His canon 'gainst self-slaughter;

or again—

> But if it be a sin to covet honour
> I am the most offending soul alive.

But I really do not know how this indescribable matter can be better described than by simply saying this; that Milton's religion was Milton's religion, and that Shakespeare's religion was not Shakespeare's.

Shakespeare never went to a public school, nor (as far as anybody knows) to any school. Milton did go to a public school; he went to the school already prophetically illuminated with my own presence. Shakespeare never went to an English University; Milton did. Milton regarded the trick of rhyming with contempt; Shakespeare used it even in the most inappropriate moments. Milton had no humour; Shakespeare had very much too much: he never lets anything else entirely run away with him, but he lets his laughter run away with him; he is sometimes absolutely incomprehensible from the incoherence of his mere animal spirits. Milton was probably unkind to his wife; Shakespeare's wife was probably unkind to him. Milton started from the very first with a clear idea of somehow making poetry. Shakespeare started with a very vague idea of somehow making money. Whenever Milton speaks of religion, it is Milton's religion: the religion that Milton has made. Whenever Shakespeare speaks of religion (which is jolly seldom) it is of a religion that has made him.

If from the above the reader cannot form a mental picture of the two men, I am sorry for him. If, however, these strictly historical facts are inadequate, I can conceive of hypothetical facts that might explain the matter. An amusing romance might be written about the everlasting adventures of the ghosts of Shakespeare and Milton passing through the world of today. . . . Milton would be regarded everywhere as an aristocrat, except among the aristocracy; Shakespeare would be regarded everywhere as a bounder, except among the aristocracy.

Many people have wondered why Milton described the Devil so much better than he described anything else. I think the reason is really simple: it is because he was so extraordinarily like the Devil himself. A certain Cavalier, whom some Puritan had denounced for the immorality of his troopers, replied (in a sentence that is none the worse for being certainly historical): "Our men had the sins of men—wine and wenching; yours had the sins of devils—spiritual pride and rebellion." I sympathize, politically speaking, with the republicanism of men like Milton; but I cannot help feeling that there was a truth in that answering taunt, and that the rebellion of Milton, at least was the rebellion of spiritual pride; it was a cold anger, an intellectual violence. I do not blame him for helping Charles I to lose his head, but I do blame him for never losing his own. This strain of a stern and frigid propriety, full of scholarly memories and many dignified public virtues, does exist in Milton and it does exist still in England. Miltonic England has nearly destroyed Merry England, but not quite. The struggle is still going on, and Shakespeare is still alive, and with him all the Middle Ages. The war in us is still going on between Falstaff, who did evil stupidly, and Satan, who desired evil intelligently. Falstaff is a mocker because he is incomplete: Satan is serious because he is complete.

For this reason it is impossible not to feel a kind of mischievous pleasure in the fact that Shakespeare escaped all those formative influences which have made the modern English gentleman. Shakespeare is a sort of gigantic truant. He ran away from school and college—at least, he kept away from school and college, and I fancy he has kept away from most of his own celebrations. The lack of biographical detail about him is not, I think, a mere accident of circumstances or records. It is a part of a certain splendid vagrancy and vagueness in the daily existence of that kind of man. We do not know much of the life of Shakespeare; but I doubt if Shakespeare knew much either. Life does not consist of incidents; incidents, even happy incidents, are often an interruption to life. It may be that Shakespeare stopped living for a moment even to imagine Othello; in such a great vitality the greatest experiences are often shapeless, unconscious and unrecorded; and it may be that the happiest hour of Shakespeare was when he had forgotten his own name. In fact, he may very well have forgotten it quite often, as he never seems to have managed to spell it twice the same. But for this reason, there must always be, as I have said, something just slightly artificial about all pomps and mysteries which celebrate Shakespeare at a particular time or in a particular place. The cant saying that Shakespeare is for all time has a double truth in it; it means that he is the kind of poet to endure for ever, and it also means that he was probably the kind of man who never knew what the time was. As Orlando says to Rosalind, "There is no clock in the forest." And as it is with time, so it is with space. Shakespeare does not live in the forests of Warwickshire, but in the forest of Arden. His traces may be found anywhere or nowhere; he is omnipresent, and yet he has escaped. He is hidden away somewhere under nameless woods, concealed along with the soul of England, where God has hidden it from imperialists and thieves.

The Great Shawkspear Mystery

I have constantly defended Mr. Bernard Shaw from the entirely frivolous charge of frivolity; I shall not, therefore, be in any danger of finding my complaint classed with the commonplace attacks upon him which represent him as a mountebank or a perverse jester if I animadvert upon his attitude on the subject of Shakespeare—an attitude which he has always professed with a considerable consistence and regularity, but of which he gave recently a rather special example in a lecture. Indeed, the two points of view do not contradict, but rather corroborate, each other. Mr. Shaw does not highly admire or profoundly enjoy Shakespeare and this is not because Mr. Shaw is frivolous, but, on the contrary, because Mr. Shaw is serious. The fault of Mr. Shaw as a philosopher or a critic of life (for every philosopher or critic of life may be allowed to have a fault) is altogether on the side of being too grave, too stern, too fanatical, too unbending and austere.

Mr. Bernard Shaw is too serious to enjoy Shakespeare. Mr. Bernard Shaw is too serious properly to enjoy life. Both these things are illogical where he is logical, chaotic where he is orderly, mystical where he is clear. In all the great Elizabethan writers there is present a certain thing which Mr. Shaw, with all his astonishing abilities, does not really understand—exuberance, an outrageous excess of words, a violent physical pleasure in mere vocabulary, an animal spirit in intellectual things. The moderns, to do them justice, are not realists. They are not under any influence from the babyish notion that art should imitate life. They realize pretty clearly that it is the business of art to exaggerate life. But they are used to seeing life (in the modern books) exaggerated in the direction of pain or sensibility or differentiation or mystery or delicacy or despair or candour or cruelty; they are well used to seeing life exaggerated in all these directions. But they are not used to seeing life exaggerated in the direction of life. That is why the moderns do not like Dickens. That is why Mr. Bernard Shaw does not like Shakespeare.

But the case of Shakespeare, and of all the men who belong to the age and spirit of Shakespeare, is, I admit a much harder one, especially for the fastidious modern mind, than any case like the case of Dickens. Dickens was always to some extent successful, even at his worst, along a line of neat and obvious facetiousness; but the great men of the Renaissance were sometimes so exuberant and exultant in their mere joy of existence that their mirth is not even obvious, and not even facetious. These giants are shaken with a mysterious laughter. They seem torn by the agony of jokes as incommunicable as the wisdom of the gods. Dickens was sometimes vulgar; he was sometimes quite fatuous and inept, but amusing he always was. But Shakespeare was sometimes too much amused even to be amusing. He is writing so much to please himself that he not only does not succeed in pleasing us, but does not even in any sense try to do so. Sometimes he seems like Rabelais, and indeed like all the humanistic comedians of the Renaissance, to be, as it were, raging at his audience in a kind of friendly fury. Now all this kind of staggering laughter and terrible plenitude of life happens to be outside Mr. Bernard Shaw's purview altogether. Mr. Bernard Shaw, as I have said before, is perfectly grave and reasonable about this matter; he is far too grave; he is too reasonable. It is not Mr. Bernard Shaw who is making game of Shakespeare at all. On the contrary, it is Shakespeare who is making game of Mr. Bernard Shaw, pelting him with preposterous words, deluging him with a kind of divine dribble, hurling at him huge jokes so simple and so stupid that only the giants can understand them.

I know quite well that this is foolishness in the eyes of

Mr. Shaw. I know quite well that he would say that this is a dribble which is by no means divine. But that is merely because what I say is true, that he has left out of him for some reason or other this almost animal joy of self-expression which is the main basis of all song. A great many of the most able and most indispensable of geniuses of the world have an advantage which arises in this way from a defect. Many very great men are most great because of some qualities that they have not got. If you suddenly took St. Paul's Cathedral off the top of Ludgate-hill we should all see the rest of Ludgate-hill with a splendid and startling clearness, as if it had been made that moment, as if we had never seen it before. In the same way, if we take out of the mind of a man an essential human quality, it may often happen that what we leave behind is sometimes something like inspiration. A prophet may sometimes be an ordinary man minus an ordinary quality. Thus, Schopenhauer saw the vast cosmic unity of the will to live outside him for the simple reason that he had not got it inside him. Thus, Carlyle made it possible for us not to be contented with mere smug utilitarianism and mechanical politics, simply because he happened to be lacking in that vital and essential human quality which enables a man to be contented with anything. Thus, Maeterlinck has been enabled to express the primal fear which lies behind all living merely because he has never gained the masculine firmness, and so never lost the boyish. Thus, again Tolstoy has been enabled to see all the blows which fall on mankind by having himself an insane notion that it is wicked to strike a blow. Thus, lastly, Mr. Shaw has been enabled to give a living and startling photograph of the prose of our existence through the simple fact that, with all his talents, he does not possess an ear for its poetry. He has one half of human sanity to perfection; he has plenty of common sense. But he has not the other half of sanity at all; he has no common nonsense.

Mr. Shaw maintains that Shakespeare wrote *As You Like It*

because he found that romantic nonsense paid, and gave it its title as an expression of contempt for the public taste. I say Shakespeare wrote romantic plays because Shakespeare was romantic; and I say that romantic plays paid because Man is romantic. In these undemocratic days we cannot grasp the possibility of the great man enjoying the same things as the ordinary man. Shakespeare enjoyed the same romance as the ordinary man, just as he enjoyed the same beer. And if Mr. Shaw really wished to compare himself with Shakespeare (which I think he never did) the comparison is really very simple. Mr. Shaw may be quite as extraordinary a man as Shakespeare; but he is only an extraordinary man. Shakespeare, like all the heroes, was an extraordinary man and an ordinary man too.

As for the title "As You Like It", Mr. Shaw is reading an ingenious priggishness into what is really one of a welter of wild and careless Elizabethan titles. The point is not whether, in the Elizabethan spirit, "As you like it" means exactly the same as "What you will". The point is whether in the Elizabethan spirit either of them meant anything except a sort of hilarious bosh. Anyone who knows the Elizabethan drama knows that it is strewn with such reckless titles, and a man who tried to find a critical meaning in each of them would end in an asylum. To take the first that comes. I think there is a play called "If it be not good the devil is in it". Perhaps Mr. Shaw thinks that this is a grave expression of the author's satisfaction with his work. Mr. Shaw is so anti-Elizabethan that he makes the Elizabethans sensible even where they meant to be silly.

Mr. Shaw says that in manner nothing could be done better than *As You Like It*, but in matter he himself could never do anything so bad. When I read this, I saw suddenly how simple is the whole mistake. I can only draw Mr. Shaw's attention to the fact that *As You Like It* is poetry. What can anybody mean by talking of the matter or manner of a poem? I will give Mr. Shaw three lines out of *As You Like It*, from the exquisite and irrational song of Hymen at the end:

> Then is there mirth in heaven,
> When earthly things made even
> Atone together.

Limit the matter to the single incomparable line, "When earthly things made even." And I defy Mr. Shaw to say which is matter and which is manner. The matter is quite as artistic as the manner, and the manner is quite as solid and spiritual as the matter. The meaning is essential to the words; the words would not be so good if they happened to mean, "There are six tom-cats in the back garden." But the words are quite equally essential to the meaning. If the words, "When earthly things made even" were presented to us in the form of "When terrestial affairs are reduced to an equilibrium," the meaning would not merely have been spoilt, the meaning would have entirely disappeared. The identity between the matter and the manner is simply the definition of poetry. The aim of good prose words is to mean what they say. The aim of good poetical words is to mean what they do not say. When Shakespeare says (in one of the long philosophical speeches which Mr. Shaw does not quote because they do not happen to be pessimistic),

> For valour, is not Love a Hercules,
> Still climbing trees in the Hesperides?

it is difficult or rather impossible to use any other language to express what he conveys. You cannot convey a sense of sunrise and an ancient hope and the colours of the ends of the earth. But if Mr. Shaw thinks that the lines mean, "is not the sexual instinct like Hercules in the matter of valour, and is it not like him in the garden of the Hesperides and climbing a tree?" I can assure him most sincerely of his mistake.

With Mr. Shaw's contention that Shakespeare was not primarily a very positive teacher, or even a man with a very definite doctrinal view of life, I am somewhat disposed to agree. To live in the thick of the Renaissance and the Reformation was to live in the thick of a scepticism and philosophical confusion as great, if not greater, than our own. He had a great deal of traditional and inherent religious emotion, and what there was of it was mainly Catholic. He talked a great deal of rather futile rhetorical scepticism, and all that was purely Renaissance. With some such reservations I should agree with Mr. Shaw if he said that Shakespeare had no philosophical creed. But I disagree with him entirely when he attempts to represent that Shakespeare had the wrong philosophical mood. I deny altogether that Shakespeare was a pessimist; the worst that you can say of him is that he was a poet.

The instance chosen by Mr. Shaw to prove the pessimism of Shakespeare, the "out brief candle" soliloquy, seems a curious instance to select. Surely it cannot have escaped Mr. Shaw that this speech has a special and definite dramatic value, a dramatic value so special and definite that it absolves one from all necessity to find in it any philosophical meaning at all. It is a speech by Macbeth just before his defeat and destruction; that is to say, it is a speech made by a wicked and wasted human soul confronted with his own colossal failure. If Shakespeare had been as much of an optimist as Walt Whitman, and had wished to make that play artistic, he would have made that speech pessimistic. The speech is not a metaphysical statement at all; it is an emotional exclamation. Mr. Shaw has no right to call Shakespeare a pessimist for having written the words "out, out, brief candle"; he might as well call Shakespeare a champion of the ideal of celibacy for having written the words, "Get thee to a nunnery." He might as well call Shakespeare a philosophical apologist for the duel for having written the words, "Kill Claudio". It is not Shakespeare's fault that, having to write pessimism for the purpose of a theatrical point, he happened to write much better pessimism than the people who are silly enough to be pessimists.

I could find many speeches in Shakespeare, philosophical or semi-philosophical, criticisms of life or descriptions of humanity, which have the happier note, and could be set over against the soliloquy of Macbeth—Biron's speech on love in *Love's Labour Lost*, several speeches of Portia, one of Orlando, and so on. But I do not think that I should attach much importance to them, any more than I attach much importance to the speeches called pessimistic. I do not think that Shakespeare meant any of these speeches as statements of his complete convictions. I am not sure whether in this exact sense he had any complete convictions. But another thing he had which is worth a word in conclusion. He had an atmosphere or spirit—an atmosphere not confined to him but common in some degree to the whole of the England before the Puritans. And about this atmosphere or spirit there is one particular thing to be remarked. It can be remarked best by simply reading such a play as *A Midsummer Night's Dream*. The quality I mean may be called the comic supernatural. The greater part of that world, like the more thinking part of our modern world, believed in a general way in the existence of things deeper and higher than man himself, in energies behind his energy, in destinies beyond his ken. In short, they believed in gods, in devils; and they also believed in fairies. We have mysticism in the modern world, but all our mysticism is sad mysticism; at the best it is serious mysticism; it is never a farcical mysticism. We believe in devils most firmly of the three; that can easily be seen in our sombre modern fiction. We believe in gods to some extent—in moderation. But it is our tendency, or has been until lately our tendency, not to believe in fairies with a proper firmness. We never think of any energies in the universe being actually merrier than we; though it comes quite easy to us to think of energies which are grimmer. In this larger and looser sense, then, Shakespeare, or rather Shakespeare's England, was the very reverse of pessimistic. It thought of the universe itself as being capable of a sort of lightness. It thought sometimes of the world itself as going round like a boy's humming-top. Now, if we dream of the ultimate mysteries the effect is generally at least a sombre one. Our Midsummer Night's Dream is uncommonly like a nightmare.

Shakespeare and Shaw

Many critics of my own modest writings, as I have had occasion to note elsewhere, have charged me with an excessive love of alliteration. To these it would be apparent that the subject of Shakespeare and Shaw has been created out of the void to satisfy this appetite, whichever of the two surnames I am supposed to have invented or assimilated to the other. Of course there is always the possibility of avoiding it by saying that the works of Shakespeare were written by Bacon; or (what seems to me rather more probable) the works of Shaw written by Sidney Webb. But the truth is, of course, that the two names have been brought together long ago by the deliberate and provocative policy of the bearer of one of them. Shaw has frequently compared himself with Shakespeare; Shakespeare was so unfortunate as to have few opportunities of comparing himself with Shaw. This was perhaps what some of the Shavians have meant by saying that Shakespeare wrote under the disadvantages of his age. This may be, in some respects, true; but it is less universally recognized that Shakespeare wrote under all the advantages of his age and Shaw under all the almost crushing disadvantages of his.

The real truth about this is as much obscured by the conventional or authoritarian appreciation of Shakespeare as by any pert or juvenile depreciation of Shakespeare; let alone depreciation of Shaw. The view of those who professed to be most disgusted at the Shavian impertinence of twenty years ago, the view of those who constituted themselves the guardians of the sacred Swan of Avon against the impudent little boy to whom all swans were geese—this view was in fact equally mistaken about the older and the younger dramatists, about the poet and about the critic. The swan was none the less a swan because, having sung its swan-song and died, it was worshipped largely by geese. But the point is that the whole conception in both cases was wrong. The conservatives regarded Shakespeare as a sort of earnest and elevating Modern Thinker, with a Noble Brow; a hero according to Carlyle and talking in the grand style as laid down by Matthew Arnold. And that was all wrong. The same conservatives regarded Bernard Shaw as a flippant and frivolous mocker of all holy things, refusing to kiss the Pope's toe and preferring to pull the poet's leg. And that was all wrong. To sum it up in two pretty adequate parallels; they made the appalling mistake of supposing that Shakespeare was like Goethe and of supposing that Shaw was like Mephistopheles. But Shakespeare was not a German, in spite of the unbiassed conclusion of German scholarship in the matter; he was the very last man in the world to be cut out for a German hero or a German god. And Shaw is not a devil; far less an imp. The truth is that of the two, it is Shakespeare who is frivolous, or who is at least capable of being irresponsible and gay. It is Shaw, in spite of his real humour, who is much more cut out to be a Goethe, an earnest sage and seer, worshipped by German audiences.

The reason of the greater richness and depth of Shakespeare's gaiety, when he is gay, is in the fact that he came at the end of an epoch of civilization and inherited, however indirectly, all the best of a very ancient culture. The reason for the greater earnestness, or what might even be called the sharper morality, in Shaw and some modern moralists, is that they came after a sort of barbaric interruption that had cut off the countries of the north from Classicism and from Humanism. Goethe was serious, because he had to struggle to recover the lost civilization for the Germans. He had to stretch himself in order to balance and stagger before he could stand upright. But Shakespeare, though he had small Latin and less Greek, had much more in him of the Greek spirit and the Latin order than most of the moderns have ever had; because he received it through a tradition and an atmosphere that had been clear and uninterrupted for some time. For instance, all that light Renaissance pessimism is perfectly incomprehensible to our heavy realistic pessimists. Schopenhauer or Hardy would never be able to understand how cheerfully an Elizabethan said that all roses must fade or that life is brief as a butterfly. Modern sceptics could never understand the subtlety and spiritual complexity with which a Humanist of that age will be talking one moment about Adonis or Apollo, as if they really existed, and the next moment be acknowledging, like Michael Angelo in his last sonnets, that nothing truly exists except Christ upon the Cross. The modern free-thinkers are more simple and in a sense more serious than this. It is they who say that life is real, life is earnest; though curiously enough it is now generally they who go on to say that the grave is certainly its goal.

The Renaissance came late to England, and Shakespeare came late even in the English Renaissance. Only the brilliant accident of a still more belated inheritor, John Milton, makes Shakespeare seem to us to stand somewhere in the middle. But the Humanism, the Hellenism and the pagan mythology mixed with Catholic theology, upon which he fed, had been flowing together from their Italian fountains since the fifteenth century; and long before those great voices of antiquity, the voice of Virgil in poetry and of Aristotle in philosophy, had spoken directly to the whole Christendom of the Middle Ages. Shakespeare was therefore familiar with a mixture of all sorts of moods, memories and fancies, and was not sharply hostile to any of them, save perhaps a little to the Puritans. He could consider a Republican hero of Plutarch, a medieval king, shining with the sacred chrism as with a nimbus, a pagan misanthrope cursing the world, a Franciscan friar cheerfully and charitably reuniting lovers, a god of the Greek oracles, a goblin of the English country lanes, a fool who was happy or a wise man who was foolish—all without setting one against the other, or thinking there was any particular conflict in the traditions; or asking himself whether he was Classic or Romantic or Medievalist or Modernist or black or white or buff or blue. Culture was not one strained agony or controversy. That is what I mean by a man inheriting a whole civilization and having the immense advantage of being born three hundred years ago.

By the time that Bernard Shaw was born, the national and religious divisions of Europe had been dug so deep, and had so long sustained what was at once a vigilant rivalry and a fight in the dark, that this sort of varied and varying balance had become almost impossible. European culture was no longer a many-coloured and stratified thing; it had been split into great fragments by earthquakes. Whatever virtues it might possess, and in a man like Bernard Shaw it does possess some of the most vital of all public virtues, it had produced that curious sort of concentration which did in fact bring forth, first the Shakespearian idolatry by the end of the eighteenth century, and then the Shavian iconoclasm by the end of the nineteenth. Both were not only serious, but entirely serious; in other words, neither was really Shakespearian. Hence arises the paradox upon which I would remark here; that the relations between the idol and the iconoclast are really the very opposite to those which seemed obvious to the idolaters in the days of my youth. It is rather Mr. Bernard Shaw who really has the gravity of the god, or at least of the prophet or oracle of the god, seeing visions of the future and speaking words of the fate of nations. And it is really Shakespeare who passes by in the woods with the elusive laughter of a Faun, and a mystery that has something of mockery.

Part Five: Review of Criticism

Professor Bradley on Shakespearian Tragedy

Professor Bradley's critical work is nearly always of that rare and excellent kind that leaves the subject as inexhaustible as it found it. The only test that can be adequately suggested of a critic's work on a masterpiece is whether it freshens it or makes it stale, whether, like the inferior appreciation, it sends us to our hundredth reading of the work, or whether, like the higher appreciation, it sends us to our first reading of it. There is one kind of criticism which reminds us that we have read a book; there is another and better which convinces us that we have never read it. Mr. Bradley's comments can almost everywhere be praised for the supreme merit that they leave us not only interested, but what is almost the same thing, unsatisfied. Infinities of argument, of agreement, of violent disagreement, of qualification and exaggerative development, could be extracted from almost every sentence. He deals with each subject firmly, but yet in such a manner as to suggest indescribably that the subject is a subject for discussion. It may, perhaps, be wondered whether one could possibly say a worse thing of anybody than that he had said "the last word" on a subject. A man who says the last word on a subject ought to be killed. He is a murderer; he has slain a topic. The best kind of critic draws attention not to the finality of a thing, but to its infinity. Instead of closing a question, he opens a hundred; he creates his enemies as much as his admirers. If any of us should meet a man walking about and claiming to say the last word on tragedy let us also take tragic action and let it be his last word on anything.

Professor Bradley realizes to the full the depth and the delicacy and the darkness of his subject; and realizing this, he contrives to say some very admirable things about it.

Nothing, for instance, could be better or sounder than this:

"The tragic hero, with Shakespeare, then, need not be 'good', though generally he is 'good', and therefore at once wins sympathy in his error. But it is necessary that he should have so much of greatness in his error that we may be vividly conscious of the possibilities of human nature. Hence, in the first place, a Shakespearian tragedy is never, like some miscalled tragedies, depressing. No one ever closes the book with the feeling that man is a poor mean creature. He may be wretched and he may be awful, but he is not small. His lot may be heartrending and mysterious, but it is not contemptible. The most confirmed of cynics ceases to be a cynic while he reads these plays. . . . It forces the mystery upon us and it makes us realize so vividly the worth of that which is wasted that we cannot possibly seek comfort in the reflection that all is vanity."

That is both profound and simple and strong. I do not quite understand why the word "good" should be printed in inverted commas, as if were some new and curious piece of slang. . . . Nor can I agree for a moment with Professor Bradley in the view he takes of Richard II, in a note appended to the passage. He says that Richard II is, in his view, an exception to this general rule of dignity and value in character, that to him Richard is "scarcely a tragic figure, he is so only because his fall from prosperity to adversity is so great". Surely this is a very unfair and unappreciative view of the personality of Richard II. Richard may be what is called a weak man, but in that respect he is only in the spiritual position essential to the protagonist of tragedy. The whole meaning of tragedy is that every man is of necessity a weak man. A poet may lawfully take a particularly weak man and symbolize the general weakness of the human estate, just as he may lawfully take a particularly sad tale to symbolize the general sadness of the human lot. But if Richard II be weak in the sense that Hamlet is weak, he is also great in the sense that Hamlet is great—nay, he is strong in the sense that Hamlet is strong. Shakespeare has given him every quality that can set off and blazon misfortune, grace, eloquence, culture, and personal courage. He has not only given him the manners of a gentleman, he has in some sense given him the death of a hero. The hired brute who strikes him down, fighting against odds, calls him as he dies "as full of valour as of noble blood". Above all, Shakespeare cannot surely have meant nothing when he poured out pages of his most superb poetry from the mouth of this man. The truth surely is that the tragedy of Richard II is the tragedy not of the King, but of the poet. Who would care how many times a dull fellow like Henry Bolingbroke won or lost his crown? The loss of a practical scheme is in its nature a trifle; it is only when it is idealized by the human imagination that it becomes a vision and hence a tragedy. The poet is a man who can value passionately the things about him, he is the man to whom the near things are not too near to be seen. He can focus them in some way; so that even the men who walk about in the room with him are seen, as it were, afar off from a peak and with a sudden cry.

Most poets, happily for them, are poor and live the life of common men. Thus the things which they make necessary to their imaginations are generally human or ordinary things. They see the poetry of the grass or of women or of bread or wine. But this unhappy man in Shakespeare was a man who was born in a crown, and his curse was that he saw the poetry of that. The trumpets blown before him were to him what the birds were to Keats or Tennyson.

The crimson canopy over his head was to him what the vault of heaven was to Shelley. Most kings are happy, because most kings are commonplace men, and being commonplace men they laugh at kingship as all commonplace men and all common sense men laugh at it. But Richard II in Shakespeare is so uncommon a King as actually to reverence his crown. His story, like that of Charles I, is simply the tragedy of Divine Right. It is safe enough (with reasonable precautions) to be a King; but it is very dangerous to be a King who is also a Royalist.

I have said above that Professor Bradley's book teems with suggestions and provocations in every sentence, and I have proved it by going off into an argument with him about a note. Properly understood, it is an excellent compliment, though it may not be an excellent advertisement. Of the four tragedies treated in the book, that which is handled in the most masterly manner is, I think, "King Lear". The study of the character of Edgar, to take one example, with its suggestion of the subtle, but essential, connection between religious faith and a kind of cheerfulness which seems almost inhuman, is one of those fine studies of normal psychology through which psychology almost becomes philosophy. Professor Bradley strikes a deep note in touching on Edgar's strange and innocent faith in "the clearest gods" amid all the monstrous darkness. It is an unconscious hypocrisy of the world and worldlings to say that they are angry with the gloom and asceticism of religious people. What they are and always have been angry with is their happiness.

A Shakespeare Portrait

It is very interesting to learn that they have found Shakespeare's portrait in a tavern, especially as that is very much the place where they would have found Shakespeare. I have no knowledge, nor even any comprehension, of the subtle and minute method by which gentlemen who are art experts are enabled to say apparently for certain what such a portrait is; but certainly there is nothing at all unreasonable in the idea of Shakespeare being painted by some early admirer of his on the panel of an inn, or in Shakespeare sitting still to have it painted, so long as they gave him beer enough. I see in one newspaper that a doubt has been raised about the probability of such an episode, and I gather from the context that this doubt was raised in the interests of the Bacon–Shakespeare School. I suppose that this particular Baconian thought that all portraits of Shakespeare ought to be portraits of Bacon; and if they weren't, why then, they weren't portraits of Shakespeare. There seems to be something a little mixed in this line of thought; but I have no time to unravel it now. In any case, what the Baconian said about the new portrait was this; "Does it seem very likely that the raw country youth who, practically penniless and burdened with a wife and three children, joins a band of strolling players in 1587, and is heard of the year after as earning a precarious living outside the theatre doors, and who, not until four years later, takes his first essay to the publishers, has his portrait in oils done in 1588—the presumed date of the above picture?"

There may be in this school of thought swift and splendid connections of ideas which I am too dull to follow. But I do not quite understand why having a wife and three children should prevent a man having his portrait painted. Painters do not commonly insist on their models being celibate, as if they were a sacred and separate order of monks. There is nothing to show that Shakespeare paid for it, or if he did pay for it, that he paid much; and it does not seem, on the face of it, very likely that a man would pay much for a comparatively rude painting in a wayside inn. Suppose we were talking of some man whom we knew to have been a poor actor at one time, travelling from place to place like any other actor, but whom we also knew to be a man of arresting personality, perhaps of fascination. Would there be anything improbable about some friend or flatterer of his youth having sketched him in some small town in which he stayed? It may seem a trivial matter; but it is not trivial, because it is typical. The discussion touching whether Bacon wrote Shakespeare is only important because it happens to be the battleground of two historical methods, of two kinds of judgment. In itself it matters little whether Bacon was Shakespeare or whether Shakespeare was Bacon. Shakespeare, I fancy, would not much mind being robbed of his literary achievements; and I am sure that Bacon would be delighted to be relieved of his political history and reputation. Francis Lord Verulam would have been a happier man, certainly a better and more Christian man, if he also had gone down to drink ale at Stratford; if he had begun and ended his story in an inn. As far as the individual glory of the two men goes, the two men had this, and perhaps only this, in common: that they both at the end of their lives seem to have decided that all glory is vanity. But, as I say, the real interest of the matter lies in a certain historical and controversial method of which this paragraph that I have quoted is an excellent example.

The two arguments that often clash in history may be called the argument from detail and the argument from atmosphere. Suppose a man two hundred years hence were writing about London cabmen. He might know all the details that can be gathered from all the documents; he might know the numbers of all the cabs the names of all the cabmen, the single and collective owners of all the vehicles in question, the fixed rate of pay and all the Acts of Parliament that in any way affected it. Yet he might not know the rich and subtle atmosphere of cabmen; their peculiar relations to the comfortable class who commonly employ them. He would not understand how paying the plain fare to a cabman is not the same as paying the plain fare to a tramconductor. He would not understand how when a cabman overcharges it is not quite the same as if a butcher or a baker had overcharged. He would not grasp to what extent these men regard themselves as the temporary dependants, the temporary coachmen of the wealthy; he would not understand how even their bad language is an expression of that idea of dependence on the historic generosity of gentlemen. He would not comprehend how this strange class of man contrived to be insolent without being independant. It is just such atmospheres as this that history only exists in order to make real; and it is just such atmospheres as this that nearly all history neglects. But those who say that Bacon wrote Shakespeare are, so to speak, the maniacs of this method of detail against atmosphere which is the curse of so many learned men. As a matter of fact the Bacon–Shakespeare people really are learned; they do really know an enormous amount about the period with which they are concerned. But it is all detail; and detail by itself means madness. The very definition of a lunatic is a man who has taken details out of their real atmosphere.

Here is an example. I remember long ago debating with a Baconian who said that Shakespeare could not have written the plays because Shakespeare was a countryman, and there was in the plays no close study of Nature in the modern sense—no details about how this bird builds its nest, or that flower shakes its pollen—as we get them in Wordsworth or in Tennyson. Now, the man who said this knew far more about Elizabethan literature than I do. In fact, he knew everything about Elizabethan literature except what Elizabethan literature was. If he had had even the smallest glimpse of what Elizabethan literature was he would never have dreamed of expecting any Elizabethan to write about Nature because he was brought up in the middle of it. A Renaissance poet brought up in a forest would not have written about trees any more than a Renaissance poet brought up in a pigstye would have written about pigs; he would have written about gods or not written at all. It was not a Renaissance idea to write about the homely natural history which was just outside the door. To say that Shakespeare, if he was really born at Stratford, would have written about birds and meadows, is like saying that Keats, if he was really born in London, would have written about omnibuses and draper's shops. I was bewildered by this incapacity in a more learned man than I to capture the obvious quality of a time. Then somebody made it worse by saying that Shakespeare could describe Nature in detail because he described in detail the appearance and paces of a horse—as if a horse were some shy bird that built its nest in dim English woodlands and which only a man born in Stratford could see. If there is one thing more certain about an Elizabethan gentleman than the fact that he would know nothing about Nature, it is the fact that he would know all about horses.

I merely quote this old example as an instance of the entire absence of a sense of historical atmosphere. That horse who built his nest in the high trees of Stratford is typical of all this unnatural criticism; the critic who found him did indeed find a mare's nest. Of the same kind is the argument that Shakespeare must have been a learned man like Bacon, because he had heard so much about learning, about law and mythology and old literature. This is like saying that I must be as learned as the Master of Balliol because I have heard of most of the things that he talks about; because I have heard of the debate of Nominalists and Realists, or because I have heard of the Absolute and the Relative being discussed at Balliol. Again the man misses the whole mood and tone of the time. He does not realize that Shakespeare's age was an age in which a fairly bright man could pick up the odds and ends of anything, just as I, by walking along Fleet Street, can pick up the odds and ends of anything. A man could no more live in London then and not hear about Pagan Mythology that he could live in London now and not hear about Socialism. The same solemn and inhuman incredulity which finds it incredible that a clever lad in London should pick up more than he really knew is the same that finds it incredible that he should have had his portrait painted for fun by some foolish painter in a public-house.

The truth is, I fear, that madness has a great advantage over sanity. Sanity is always careless. Madness is always careful. A lunatic might count all the railings along the front of Hyde Park; he might know the exact number of them, because he thought they were something else. A healthy man would not know the number of the railings, or perhaps even the shape of the railings; he would know nothing about them except the supreme, sublime, Platonic, and transcendental truth, that they were railings. There is a great deal of falsehood in the notion that truth must necessarily prevail. There is this falsehood to start with: that if a man has got the truth he is generally happy. And if he is happy he is generally lazy. The incessant activity, the exaggerated intelligence, generally belong to those who are a little wrong and just a little right. The whole advantage of those who think that Bacon wrote Shakespeare lies simply in the fact that they care whether Bacon wrote Shakespeare. The whole disadvantage of those who do not think it lies in the fact that (being folly) they do not care about it. The sane man who is sane enough to see that Shakespeare wrote Shakespeare is the man who is sane enough not to worry whether he did or not.

Madame de Chambrun on Shakespeare

I have recently read with very great interest a book on the subject of Shakespeare's Sonnets, of the Dark Lady and the poet's relation to Southampton and Essex and Bacon and various eminent men of his time. The book is by the Comtesse de Chambrun and it seems to me both fascinating and convincing. I hasten to say that the lady is very learned and I am very ignorant. I do not profess to know much about Shakespeare, outside such superfluous trifling as the reading of his literary works. Madame de Chambrun's book is called *Shakespeare, Actor-Poet*; and I must humbly confess that I have known him only in his humbler capacity as a poet, and have never devoted myself to the more exhausting occupation of studying all the green-room gossip about him as an actor. But it is very right that more scholarly people should study the biographical problem; and even a poor literary critic may be allowed to judge their studies as literature. And this study seems to me to be one very valuable to literature; and not, like so many of the Baconian penny-dreadfuls, a mere insult to literature. Indeed some Baconian books are quite as much of an insult to Bacon as to Shakespeare. I have no authority to decide the controversies of fact raised here, about the relation of Southampton to the Sonnets or the discovery of the Dark Lady in the family of Davenant. I can only say that to a plain man the arguments seem at least to be of a plain sort. Thus, I have never had any reason to quarrel with Mr. Frank Harris or Mr. Bernard Shaw about the claims of Miss Mary Fitton, or to break a lance for or against that questionable queen of beauty. I have lances enough to break with them about more important things. But to my simplicity it does seem rather notable that next to nothing is known about the Dark Lady except that she was dark, and precious little seems to be known about Mary Fitton except that she was fair. Or again, I profess myself utterly incompetent to consider the question of what "T.T." meant by "W.H."; and I do not think the difficulty will interfere very much with my joy in saying to myself, "But thine immortal beauty shall not fade", or, "Give not a windy night a rainy morrow". But if it be true, as it is here stated, that some of these sonnets were already written when William Herbert, Lord Pembroke, was only eleven years old, he certainly must have been a precocious child if what Shakespeare says about him is at all appropriate. There may be ingenious answers to these things that I do not know. But to guileless ignorance like my own the point seems rather a practical one. As a matter of fact, I have generally found in these cases that the ingenious explanations were a little too ingenious. But, as I have said, I have no intention of dogmatizing on these problems.

Madame de Chambrun's theory is that the young man for whom Shakespeare had such a hero-worship was his own patron and protector, the Earl of Southampton, for whom indeed she has some little hero-worship herself. But she gives very good and convincing grounds for regarding him as something of a hero. I am pretty sure she is quite right in saying that the rebellion of Essex and Southampton was essentially just and public-spirited. She says that if it had succeeded they would have been handed down to all history as patriots and reformers. I am also quite sure she is right in saying that it was rather a rebellion against Cecil than against Elizabeth that alone would make it creditable. It is curious to note that, in this account, Bacon and Shakespeare, so far from being conspirators and collaborators, were two antagonistic figures in two opposite factions; one on each side of a serious civil war. Bacon was the bitter accuser of Essex; indeed, Bacon had probably become a sort of hack and servant of Cecil. Shakespeare was of course a friend and follower of Southampton, who was a friend and follower of Essex. According to this account, Shakespeare was presenting plays like *Richard II* as deliberate political demonstrations, designed to warn weak sovereigns of the need of greater wisdom, at the very time when Bacon was drawing up the heads of his detailed and virulent denunciation of the rebel. However this may be, it is practically certain that there was the chasm between the two great men, whom some have blended into one great man (we might say into one great monster). This theory would make an even stranger monster of the Baconian version of Bacon. Not only was he capable of leading two separate public lives, but even of figuring in two opposite political parties. He must have been plotting against himself all night and condemning himself to be hanged on the following day.

If I say that this fancy would turn Bacon and Shakespeare into Jekyll and Hyde, the partisans of the two parties will probably dispute rather eagerly about which was which. But I for one have very little doubt on that point. And I am glad to find that Madame de Chambrun thinks very much the same and knows very much more. If ever there was a base business in human history, it was the method of government which Burleigh and his son conducted in England in the name of Elizabeth, and, I am sorry to say, to some extent with the assistance of Bacon. The people whom Robert Cecil destroyed were all more honest than himself (not that that was saying much) and some of them were sufficiently honourable and spirited to dwarf his little hunchbacked figure even by their dignity in the hour of death. Whether it were Essex or Mary Stuart or even poor Guy Fawkes, they might have stood on the scaffold only in order to make him look small. And I am heartily glad to hear, if it be true, that this nest of nasty plutocrats, with Cecil in the midst of it, counted among its enemies the greatest of Englishmen. It gives me great pleasure to think that it was of those Tudor politicians that he was thinking, when he talked of strength by limping away disabled, and art made tongue-tied by authority and captive good attending captain ill. The last line must have described a good many scenes on the scaffold in the sixteenth century. It may be difficult to imagine Shakespeare greater than Shakespeare. But it is possible that if his friends had triumphed and his cause and faith revived, he might in some unthinkable transfiguration have been greater than himself.

I know much less of the other problem involved, which is entirely one of private life and not of public policy. I mean the question of that mysterious and sinister woman towards whom the sonneteer revives the ancient rage of inconsistencies; the *odi et amo* of Catullus. But even I, as a mere casual reader of things in general, had certainly heard of the joke or scandal which is said to have suggested Sir William Davenant was a natural son of William Shakespeare. Whether this was so or not, Shakespeare certainly knew the Davenants, who kept an inn where he visited and where (as the writer of this book explains) Southampton himself appeared on the scene at a later stage. Madame de Chambrun's theory is that Mrs. Davenant was what we should now call a vamp; that she had at one time vamped the poet and went on later to vamp the peer. But the poet, though his feelings were mixed, could already see through the lady and was furious at the duping of his friend; and out of this triple tangle of passions came the great tragic sequence of the Sonnets. Upon this I cannot pronounce, beyond repeating that it is set out in this book with great cogency, comprehension, and grip; and without a trace of that indefinable disproportion and lack of balance, which makes many learned and ingenious works on such subjects smell faintly of the madhouse. The writer keeps control of the subject; we feel that, though her conclusions are definite, she would not be seriously upset if they were definitely disproved. She appeals to facts and fairness throughout; and nobody can do more. The documentation and system of references seems to be very thorough; and, in a matter which I am better able to judge, there is nowhere

that sense of strain in the argument, or of something altogether far-fetched in the explanation which continually jars
us in most reconstructions of this kind, especially in the dangerous era of Elizabeth. Perhaps after all, that era really was
the great spiritual battle; and Shakespeare and Bacon really
were the spirits that met in conflict. But anyhow, it is a queer
paradox that Shakespeare was an obscure and almost unhis-
torical figure; according to some nameless or worthless,
according to others impersonal and self-effacing; but
anyhow somewhat elusive and secret; and from him came a
cataract of clear song and natural eloquence, while Bacon
was a public man of wide renown and national scientific
philosophy, and out of him have come riddles and oracles
and fantastic cryptograms and a lifelong hobby for lunatics.

More Gammon of Bacon

For some reason not very easy to discover, books on the Bacon–Shakespeare controversy continue to be produced in great numbers and voluminous form, although the case for the Baconian cypher has been irremediably damaged by Mr. Sidney Lee's critique of Mrs. Gallup, and finally shattered to pieces by Mrs. Gallup's reply. I have read the mass of these works as they appeared down to the latest, *The Problem of the Shakespeare Plays* by Mr. George C. Bompas, and the general impression produced upon my mind takes the form of an impassioned hope that I may never be tried for my life before a jury of Baconians. If the average judge or jury treated evidence as the Baconians treat it there is not one of us who might not be in hourly peril of being sent to prison for bigamy or embezzlement or piracy on the high seas. In order to show that any one of us was identical with some celebrated criminal nothing would be necessary except to show that we had once or twice used the same popular turns of expression. The most harmless householder in London might on the Baconian method be suddenly convicted of having committed the Whitechapel murders, and the evidence might be that one of his cousins was in the habit of calling him "Jack" and that some slangy friend of his had in an authenticated letter described him as "a ripper". Some people may fancy that this is an exaggerated parallel. Let me merely quote in answer one of the actual arguments of Mr. G. C. Bompas:

"The moon so constant in inconstancy."
—Bacon: Trans. Psalm civ

"Oh, swear not by the moon, the inconstant moon.'
—Romeo and Juliet

It is seriously argued that two men must be the same man because they both employ the expression "the inconstant moon". I suppose that all the poems in all the ages which contain the expression, "rosy dawn" were all secretly written by the same man.

If education is to be seriously remodelled and set upon larger foundations in our age, surely one branch of the mind to which more attention should be given is the power of valuing evidence. Almost every one of the books which have passed before me in this matter display an absolute inability to realize what is significant and what is insignificant in a human problem. There ought to be a series of textbooks on evidence and arguments as to probability, in all the schools. In the simpler textbooks would be found the general principles of which the Baconians stand in need. For instance, children would be made to learn by heart the following rules:

I. To establish a connection between two persons, the points of resemblance must be not only common to the two individuals but must not be common to any large number of persons outside. Example: Thus it is no evidence of connection between Jones and Brown that they both put money on the Derby, or that they both at one particular period of London life said, "There's 'air."

II. Similarly, it is no proof of the connection between two persons that they both do something which, though it may not actually be done by many people might at any moment be done by anybody. Example: Thus it is no proof of connection between Jones and Brown that they both sneezed twice on a Thursday morning, or that they both had a door-knocker carved with the head of a lion.

III. In order to establish a connection between two men it is necessary that the points of resemblance should be (a) characteristics, having something of the actual colour of an individual's character, (b) things in themselves unusual or difficult or dependent on a particular conjunction of events, (c) things, generally speaking, which it is easier to imagine one man only at a particular time doing, or two men conspiring to do, than to imagine two or more men at that time independently and simultaneously doing. Example: Thus a connection would be established between Jones and Brown, though only to a limited extent, if Brown were the only Cabinet Minister in the same social circle with Jones, and Jones had learnt a Cabinet secret.

These rules of evidence are so simple and obvious that at first sight it may seem a waste of time to summarize them even briefly. But if a reader will apply them steadily through the whole of one of the Baconian books, he will find it may be said without the least exaggeration that by the end of the process every vestige of the book has vanished.

To quote examples of this in full would be to quote the whole book. I may, however, give the following instances in order to show that I do not overstate the case:

"His purpose was to break the knot of the conspiracy,"
—*History of Henry V*

This sentence from Bacon is gravely paralleled with the line from *The Merry Wives of Windsor*:

"There's a knot, a gin, a conspiracy against me."

Again we have:

"Wretches have been able to stir up earthquakes by the murdering of princes."
—*Bacon's charge against Owen*

"Wherefore this ghastly looking. What's the matter?
Oh! 'twas a din to fright a monster ear
to make an earthquake."
—*Tempest*

" 'Ordinatis belli et pacis est absoluti imperii,' a principal flower

of the crown. For if those flowers should wither and fall, the garland will not be worth the wearing."—*Report 606. Bacon.*

Catesby: "Till Richard wear the garland of the realm."
                                                    —*Richard III*

And it is solemnly proposed that we should believe in a
story more sensational than that of a fifth-rate historical
novel upon such evidence as this, that Bacon and Shakespeare both called a conspiracy "a knot", that they both made
an allusion to an earthquake, and both made an allusion to a
garland. If anyone will bring me two books taken at random
from a bookcase, I will undertake to find in them better
internal evidence than this that they were both written by
one man.

The remainder of Mr. Bompas's parallels may chiefly be
grouped into two classes. The first class shows that Bacon
and Shakespeare both alluded to old stories that they must
both have read. The second class shows that Bacon and
Shakespeare both alluded to theories and superstitions that
everybody in that time must have known. Will it be seriously
credited as an example of the first class that Mr. Bompas
makes capital out of the fact that both Bacon and Shakespeare refer to so old and banal a story as that of Tarquin
slashing off the heads of the poppies? Will it be believed as
an example of the second class that he makes an argument
out of the facts that Bacon refers to a toad having a jewel in its
head? It does not seem to occur to him that Shakespeare's
lines would be perfectly pointless if they did not allude to a
commonly received story. Mr. Bompas might as well
endeavour to establish a connection between all the people
who ever said that it was unlucky to sit down thirteen to table.
Most incredible of all is the fact that a man professing to
write seriously about a problem of the sixteenth century
points it out as a coincidence that Bacon and Shakespeare
both compared seditions to "evil humours" in the body,
the veriest catch-word of contemporary physiology. He might

as well identify all the people who talk about "social deca-
dence".

I have given a list of these quibbles because it is supremely
necessary to realize with what kind of matter these immense
volumes are padded; and it is not difficult to realize that
where such arguments are used there is likely to be a dearth
of better ones. Wherever Mr. Bompas uses a more general
or vital argument it is vitiated with the same underlying
evil, an absolute refusal to realize the spirit of the Elizabethan
era. Let me take a single example. Mr. Bompas argues that if
Shakespeare was in reality the author, it is extraordinary
that all the natural history in the plays is taken from old
books and stories, and none of it from the actual details of the
country round Stratford. But does Mr. Bompas really know
so little of the age about which he writes as to suppose that
any poet in that time would have taken any notice of nature,
in the modern sense, even if he had been surrounded by miles
of pigs and primroses. To notice, in the Tennysonian manner,
what colour a certain leaf turns in September, what note a
certain bird utters in spring, would have been as impossible
either to Shakespeare or Bacon as to write *The Origin of
Species*. All their natural history was traditional; and if
Shakespeare had been ten times a rustic and had never been
near London, he would have got his natural history from
tradition: he would no more have written about the habits of
the squirrel than Spenser wrote about the streets and shop-
windows of London, where he was born. Not to realize this is
to be incapable at the outset of understanding a problem of
the Renaissance.

Lastly, the general argument drawn from the historic
personality of Shakespeare shows a failure to understand
not only the time but the eternal conditions of the problem.
Mr. Bompas cannot believe that Shakespeare, a common
practical man who worked hard to better his position, who
had several perfectly solid and temporal ambitions, who
retired a rich man to Stratford and enjoyed the good things

of this life, was really the author of so many miracles of thought and language. The author must have been, according to Mr. Bompas, a man like Bacon, a man who had travelled, who had seen strange countries, who had dealt with great matters, who had known violent reverses and terrible secrets of State. With this view I venture most profoundly to disagree. There is no clearer mark, I think, of the second-rate man of genius than that he goes out to look for the world as if it were a marvellous island far away. The first-rate man of genius, like Shakespeare, sees the world in his own front garden. There is no clearer mark of the second-rate philanthropist than that he goes out to look for humanity, as if it were a race of blue apes in Central Africa. To the true philanthropist, like Shakespeare, one village is enough to show the whole drama of creation and judgment. There is no clearer mark of the second-rate poet than that he despises business. The true poet, like Shakespeare, despises nothing. Buying and selling and building a house in Stratford seem very derogatory to Mr. Bompas; they did not seem so to Shakespeare; he knew that all points on the eternal circle are equidistant from the centre.

Sensationalism and a Cipher I

The revival of the whole astonishing Bacon–Shakespeare business is chiefly interesting to the philosophical mind as an example of the power of the letter which killeth and of how finally and murderously it kills. Baconianism is, indeed, the last wild monstrosity of literalism; it is a sort of delirium of detail. A handful of printers' types, a few alphabetical comparisons are sufficient to convince the Baconians of a proposition which is fully as fantastic historically as the proposition that the Battle of Waterloo was won by Leigh Hunt disguised as Wellington, or that the place of Queen Victoria for the last forty years of her reign was taken by Miss Frances Power Cobbe. Both these hypotheses are logically quite possible. The dates agree; the physical similarity is practically sufficient. Briefly, in fact, there is nothing to be said against the propositions except that every sane man is convinced that they are untrue.

Let us consider for a moment the Baconian conception from the outside. A sensational theory about the position of Shakespeare was certain in the nature of things to arise. Men of small imagination have sought in every age to find a cipher in the indecipherable masterpieces of the great. Throughout the Middle Ages the whole of the *Aeneid*, full of the sad and splendid eloquence of Virgil, was used as a conjuring book. Men opened it at random, and from a few disconnected Latin words took a motto and an omen for their daily work. In the same way men in more modern times have turned to the Book of Revelation full of the terrible judgment, and yet more terrible consolation of a final moral arbitration, and found in it nothing but predictions about Napoleon Bonaparte and attacks on the English Ritualists. Everywhere, in short, we find the same general truth—the truth that facts can prove anything and that there is nothing so misleading as that which is printed in black and white. Almost everywhere and almost invariably the man who has sought a cryptogram in a great masterpiece has been highly exhilarated, logically justified, morally excited, and entirely wrong.

If, therefore, we continue to study Baconianism from the outside—a process which cannot do it or any other thesis any injustice—we shall come more and more to the conclusion that it is in itself an inevitable outcome of the circumstances of the case and the tendencies of human nature. Shakespeare was by the consent of all human beings a portent. If he had lived some thousand years earlier, people would have turned him into a god. As it is, people can apparently do nothing but attempt to turn him into a Lord Chancellor. But their great need must be served. Shakespeare must have his legend, his whisper of something more than common origin. They must at least make of him a mystery, which is as near as our century can come to a miracle. Something sensational about Shakespeare was bound ultimately to be said, for we are still the children of the ancient earth, and have myth and idolatry in our blood. But in this age of a convention of scepticism we cannot rise to an apotheosis. The nearest we can come to it is a dethronement.

So much for the *a priori* probability of a Baconian theory coming into existence. What is to be said of the *a priori* probability of the theory itself; or, rather, to take the matter in its most lucid order, what is the theory? In the time roughly covered by the latter part of the reign of Queen Elizabeth and the earlier part of the reign of James I, there arose a school of dramatists who covered their country with glory and filled libraries with their wild and wonderful plays. They differed in type and station to a certain extent: some were scholars, a few were gentlemen, most were actors and many were vagabonds. But they had a common society, common meeting-places, a common social tone. They

differed in literary aim and spirit: to a certain extent some
were great philosophic dramatists, some were quaint humor-
ists, some mere scribblers of a sort of half-witted and half-
inspired melodrama. But they all had a common style, a
common form and vehicle, a common splendour, and a
common error in their methods. Now, the Baconian theory is
that one of these well-known historical figures—a man who
lived their life and shared their spirit, and who happened
to be the most brilliant in the cultivation of their particular
form of art—was, as a matter of fact, an impostor, and that
the works which his colleagues thought he had written in the
same spirit and the same circumstances in which they had
written theirs, were not written by him, but by a very celebrated judge and politician of that time, whom they may
sometimes have seen when his coach-wheels splashed them as
he went by.

Now, what is to be said about the *a priori* probability of this
view, which I stated, quite plainly and impartially above?
The first thing to be said, I think, is that a man's answer to
the question would be a very good test of whether he had the
rudiments of a historical instinct, which is simply an instinct
which is capable of realizing the way in which things happen. To many this will appear a vague and unscientific way
of approaching the question. But the method I now adopt is
the method which every reasonable being adopts in dis-
tinguishing between fact and fiction in real life. What would
any man say if he were informed that in the private writings
of Lord Rosebery that statesman claimed to have written the
poems of Mr. W. B. Yeats? Certainly, he could not deny that
there were very singular coincidences in detail. How remarkable, for instance, is the name Primrose, which is obviously
akin to modest rose, and thus to "Secret Rose". On the top
of this comes the crushing endorsement of the same idea
indicated in the two words, "rose" and "bury". The remarks
of the ploughman in the *Countess Kathleen* (note the rank in the
peerage selected) would be anxiously scanned for some not

improbable allusion to a furrow; and everything else, the statesman's abandonment of Home Rule, the poet's aversion to Imperialism, would be all parts of Lord Rosebery's cunning. But what, I repeat, would a man say if he were asked if the theory was probable? He would reply, "The theory is as near to being impossible as a natural phenomenon can be. I know Mr. W. B. Yeats, I know how he talks, I know what sort of a man he is, what sort of people he lives among, and know that he is the man to have written those poems. I know Lord Rosebery too, and what sort of a life his is, and I know that he is not."

Now, we know, almost as thoroughly as we should know the facts of this hypothetical case, the facts about Bacon and Shakespeare. We know that Shakespeare was a particular kind of man who lived with a particular kind of men, all of whom thought much as he thought and wrote much as he wrote. We know that Bacon was a man who lived in another world, who thought other thoughts, who talked with other men, who wrote another style, one might almost say another language. That Bacon wrote Shakespeare is certainly possible; but almost every other hypothesis, that Bacon never said so, that he lied when he said it, that the printers played tricks with the documents, that the Baconians played tricks with the evidence, is in its nature a hundred times more probable. Of the cipher itself, I shall speak in another article. For the moment it is sufficient to point out that the Baconian hypothesis has against it the whole weight of historical circumstance and the whole of that supra-logical realization which some of us call transcendentalism, and most of us common sense.

Sensationalism and a Cipher II

In a previous article I drew attention to the general spirit in which the Baconian question must be approached. That spirit involves the instinct of culture which does not consist merely in knowing the fact, but in being able to imagine the truth. The Baconians imagine a vain thing, because they believe in facts. Their historical faculty is a great deal more like an ear for music. One of the matters, for example, which is most powerfully concerned in the Bacon–Shakespeare question is the question of literary style, a thing as illogical as the bouquet of a bottle of wine. It is the thing, in short, which makes us quite certain that the sentence quoted in *The Tragedy of Sir Francis Bacon* from his secret narrative, "The Queen looked pale from want of rest, but was calm and compos'd," was never written by an Elizabethan. Having explained the essentials of the method as they appear to me, I now come to the study of the mass of the Baconian details. They are set forth in a kind of résumé of various Baconian theories in *The Tragedy of Sir Francis Bacon* by Harold Bayley (Grant Richards). The work is an astonishing example of this faculty of putting out the fire of truth with the fuel of information. Mr. Bayley has collected with creditable industry an enormous number of fragmentary facts and rumours. He has looked at the water-marks in the paper used by the Rosicrucians and Jacobean dramatists. He has examined the tail-pieces and ornamental borders of German and Belgian printers. He has gone through the works of Bacon and Shakespeare and a hundred others, picking out parallel words and allusions, but all the time he is completely incapable of realizing the great and glaring truism which lies at the back of the whole question, the simple truism that a million times nought is nought. He does not see, that is, that though a million coincidences, each of which by itself has a slight value, may make up a probability, yet a million coincidences, each of which has no value in itself, make up nothing at all.

What are the sort of coincidences upon which Mr. Bayley relies? The water-mark used in some book is the design of a bunch of grapes. Bacon says, in the *Novum Organum*: "I pledge mankind in liquor pressed from countless grapes." Another water-mark represents a seal. Somebody said about Bacon that he became Lord Keeper of the Great Seal of England and of the great seal of nature. The rose and the lily were symbols used by the Rosicrucians; there are a great many allusions to roses and lilies in Shakespeare. A common printer's border consists of acorns. Bacon somewhere alludes to his fame growing like an oak tree. Does not Mr. Bayley see that no conceivable number of coincidences of this kind would make an account more probable or even more possible? Anyone in any age might talk about clusters of grapes or design clusters of grapes; anyone might make an ornament out of acorns; anyone might talk about growing like a tree. I look down at my own floor and see the Greek key pattern round the oilcloth, but it does not convince me that I am destined to open the doors of Hellenic mystery. Mr. Bayley undoubtedly produces a vast number of these parallels, but they all amount to nothing. In my previous article I took for the sake of argument the imaginary case of Lord Rosebery and Mr. W. B. Yeats. Does not Mr. Bayley see that to point out one genuine coincidence, as that Lord Rosebery paid secret cheques to Mr. Yeats, might indicate something, but to say that they both walked down Piccadilly, that they both admired Burne-Jones, that they both alluded more than once to the Irish question, in short that they both did a million things that are done by a million other people, does not approach even to having the faintest value or significance. This then, is the first thing to be said to the

Baconian spirit, that it does not know how to add up a column of noughts.

The second thing to be said is rather more curious. If there is a cipher in the Shakespearian plays, it ought presumably to be a definite and unmistakable thing. It may be difficult to find, but when you have found it you have got it. But the extraordinary thing is that Mr. Bayley and most other Baconians talk about the Baconian cipher as they might talk about "a touch of pathos" in Hood's poetry, or "a flavour of cynicism" in Thackeray's novels, as if it were a thing one became faintly conscious of and suspected, without being able to point it out. If anyone thinks this unfair, let him notice the strange way in which Mr. Bayley talks about previous Baconian works. "In 1888 Mr. Ignatius Donelly claimed to have discovered a cipher story in the first folio of Shakespeare's plays. In his much abused but little read and less refuted book, *The Great Cryptogram*, he endeavoured to convince the world of the truth of his theory. Partly by reason of the complexity of his system, the full details of which he did not reveal, and partly owing to the fact that he did not produce any definite assertion of authorship, but appeared to have stumbled into the midst of a lengthy narrative, the world was not convinced, and Mr. Donelly was greeted with Rabelaisian laughter. He has since gone to the grave unwept, unhonoured, and unsung, and his secret has presumably died with him. The work of this writer was marred by many extravagant inferences, but *The Great Cryptogram* is nevertheless a damning indictment which has not yet been answered." Again, on the second Baconian demonstration, "Dr. Owen gave scarcely more than a hint of how his alleged cipher worked." The brain reels at all this. Why do none of the cipherists seem to be sure what the cipher is or where it is? A man publishes a huge book to prove that there is a cryptogram, and his secret dies with him. Another man devotes another huge book to giving "scarcely more than a hint of it". Are these works really so impenetrable that no one knows whether they all revealed the same cipher or different ciphers? If they pointed to the same cipher it seems odd that Mr. Bayley does not mention it. If their ciphers were different we can only conclude that the great heart of America is passionately bent on finding a cipher in Shakespeare—anyhow, anywhere, and of any kind.

Finally, there is one thing to be said about a more serious matter. In the chapter called "Mr. William Shakespeare" the author has an extraordinary theory that Shakespeare could not have been the author of the works under discussion because those works rise to the heights of mental purity, and the little we know of Shakespeare's life would seem to indicate that it was a coarse and possibly a riotous one. "Public opinion," he says solemnly, "asks us to believe that this divine stream of song, history, and philosophy sprang from so nasty and beastly a source." There is not much to be said about an argument exhibiting so strange an ignorance of human nature. The argument could equally be used to prove that Leonardo da Vinci could not paint, the Mirabeau could not speak, and that Burns's poems were written by the parson of his parish. But surely there is no need to say this to the Baconians. They should be the last people in the world to doubt the possibility of the conjunction of genius with depravity. They trace their sublime stream of song to a corrupt judge, a treacherous friend, a vulgar sycophant, a man of tawdry aims, of cowardly temper, of public and disgraceful end. He killed his benefactor for hire, and the Baconians would improve this and say that he killed his brother. We know little of Shakespeare's vices, but he might have been a scarecrow of profligacy and remained a man worthier to create Portia than the Lord Verulam whom all history knows. The matter is a matter of evidence, and sentiment has little concern with it. But if we did cherish an emotion in the matter it would certainly be a hope that "the divine stream of song" might not be traced to "so nasty and beastly a source" as Francis Bacon.

Is Shakespeare an Allegory?

Mr. Charles Downing is the author of *God in Shakespeare*. He believes that the great dramatist was a reincarnation of the Divine. If we should freely admit that Shakespeare was divine, merely extending the remark to Homer, Aristophanes, Mr. Bradlaugh, and Mr. James Harris of Brixton, we fear that Mr. Downing would not be satisfied. It is due to him, however, to say that his work is a great improvement, in point of refinement and restraint, upon the ordinary ruck of works on what is (for some mysterious reason) called the "problem of Shakespeare"; the works which prove that he was Christ, Bacon and anyone else but himself. There are real degrees of taste even in absurdity, and it is possible for a maniac to rave with the most perfect good breeding. Mr. Downing, in propounding his outrageous thesis, has real humility and the real dignity that only comes of humility. But his attitude is vitiated to the very root by a low and inadequate conception of the nature of symbolism. He opens his book with the following remarks:

"Of recent years there has been in literature a great turning of the spirit to symbolism and to what may be called essential religion. Maeterlinck abroad and Mr. Yeats at home are the names most prominent to me, at this moment, in the movement, but it pervades literature, and the latest minor poet will show traces of its influences."

This is profoundly and most fortunately true. But Mr. Downing entirely mistakes the real nature of symbolism as evinced in Maeterlinck and Mr. Yeats when he seeks in Shakespeare for a fixed scheme of allegory. "Hermione (of *The Winter's Tale*), the ideal of the Graeco-Roman world . . . has stepped down from her pedestal, a statue come to life,

CHESTERTON ON SHAKESPEARE

and clasped in her hands Perdita, the Christian ideal." This is not the sort of thing Maeterlinck or Mr. Yeats writes, and is presumably not the sort of thing that Shakespeare wrote. Maeterlinck's characters do not represent particular cliques and schools in Belgian art and politics; they represent eternal things for which no philosophic name will ever be found. Mr. Yeats's pre-historic heroes are introduced upon the stage in order to typify elemental mysteries which cannot be typified in any other way. We need a much clearer conception of the real value and function of mysticism. It is not mysticism to explain a puzzle; to say that a green cross means evolution and a blue triangle means orthodoxy. This sort of allegorical art is a mere cryptogram which ceases to exist when it is explained. Whatever a mystic may be, he is surely not only a person who destroys mystery.

The real function of symbolism is much deeper and much more practical. We are surrounded in this world by huge and anonymous forces; as they rush by us we throw a name at them—love, death, destiny, remembrance—but the things themselves are infinitely vaster and more varied than the names. True artistic symbolism exists in order to provide another alphabet, for the direct interpretation of these infinite anarchic things, than the alphabet of language. It is not that a sea at sunset "represents" sorrow, but that a sea at sunset represents a great deal of the truth which is missed by the word "sorrow". So it is with Mr. Downing's Shakespeare allegory. It is not that Shakespeare is a mere philosopher: it is that philosophy is one way of describing certain unutterable things, and Shakespeare is another. Caliban, says Mr. Downing, "represents the mob". The truth is that Caliban represents an old, dark, and lawless element in things, an element which has no name except Caliban, and of which the mob is one of the hundred incarnations. So far from it being true that Caliban symbolizes the mob in the street, it would be far truer to say that the mob in the street symbolizes Caliban.

This errors runs through the whole conception of *The Messiahship of Shakespeare*; the poet is perpetually being made to describe, not things themselves, but the metaphysical names of things. Shakespeare was in one sense a thorough mystic; he saw in every stone in the street things which cannot be uttered till the end of the world. His Perdita is not "a type of the Reformation" but simply a girl in love; the Reformation is, in comparison, a trivial thing.

Mr. Downing's taste for turning good poetry into bad metaphysics has its humorous aspects, as where he provides precise logical translations of many of the sonnets. We give one example. A famous sonnet begins:

> Oh, how thy worth with manners may I sing
> When thou art all the better part of me?
> What can mine own praise to mine own self bring?

The following is, according to Mr. Downing, what the three lines really mean:

(1) How in modesty can I sing the worth of Beauty?
(2) When it is all my better part, my thought, my genius, my soul.
(3) What value has self-praise?

If this is really what Shakespeare meant, we can only say that literature should be everlastingly grateful that it is not what he said.

It is, however, in his treatment of *The Tempest* that Mr. Downing shows most singularly his cut-and-dried conception of allegory. For *The Tempest* really is a mystical play; its figures are symbols, but not mere mathematical symbols. Here is a description of the meaning of the wreck:

> Alonzo, the ruling class, is in despair, but still clings to Antonio and Sebastian, Ambition and *Laissez Faire*, its old vices. . . . Authority being thus divided between the Backward and progressive parties, the Mob, Caliban, lifts up its head, and, led on by Stephano and Trinculo, Sensuality and Folly, riots freely, threatening the destruction of Prospero, all Justice, Law, and Civilization, from the earth.

What is the good of this kind of symbolism? If Shakespeare meant to convey the word Ambition, why did he go to the trouble of saying the word Antonio? The truth is that Shakespeare was a symbolist of the genuine type, and symbolism of the genuine type is wholly misunderstood by Mr. Downing and his school. A real symbol of a certain law is not a mere cipher-term arbitrarily connected with that law, but an *example* of that law. A plough is symbolic of the toil of all things because it is an instance of it. The parables of the New Testament, for instance, are built wholly upon this principle; so are the one or two mystical plays of Shakespeare. It is not, as Mr. Downing would put it, that Prospero was not a man but an image of God but that he was a man, and, therefore, an image of God. The same may be said of Shakespeare. We have said nothing about this central theological theory of Mr. Downing, and our silence has been deliberate. Before we decide whether any man (even the stupidest man in the street) is God, we must take the preliminary precaution of knowing what God is and what man is.

Sources

SET IN A SILVER SEA

English Literature and the
    Latin tradition
      The Fortnightly Review,
        August 1935

The Mind of the Middle Ages
    v. The Renaissance
      Extracts from "Chaucer",
        Faber & Faber, 1932

THE TRAGEDIES

The True Hamlet
      The Speaker, June 29, 1901

Hamlet and the
    Psycho-Analyst
      "Fancies versus ads",
        Methuen, 1923

King Claudius: Dominus Rex
      Illustrated London News,
        September 12, 1925

The Orthodoxy of Hamlet
      "Lunacy and Letters",
        Sheed & Ward, 1958

The Grave-digger
      "Lunacy and Letters",
        Sheed & Ward, 1958

On a Humiliating Heresy
      "Come to Think Of It",
        Methuen, 1930

The Macbeths
      "The Spice of Life", Darwen
        Finlayson, 1964

Realism in Art
      Illustrated London News,
        March 2, 1912

The Tragedy of King Lear
      "The Spice of Life", Darwen
        Finlayson, 1964

THE COMEDIES

Shakespeare and the Legal
    Lady
      "Fancies versus Fads",
        Methuen, 1923

The Heroines of Shakespeare
      "A Handful of Authors",
        Sheed & Ward, 1953

The Repetition of Rosalind
      New York American, August 6,
        1932